7 Steps to Success in Dual Language Immersion

7 Steps

to Success in

Dual Language

Immersion

A Brief Guide for Teachers & Administrators

Lore Carrera-Carrillo & Annette Rickert Smith

Heinemann
Portsmouth, NH

Heinemann
A division of Reed Elsevier Inc.
361 Hanover Street
Portsmouth, NH 03801–3912
www.heinemann.com

Offices and agents throughout the world

Library of Congress Cataloging-in-Publication Data
Carrera-Carrillo, Lore.
    7 steps to success in dual language immersion : a brief guide for teachers and administrators /
Lore Carrera-Carrillo, Annette Rickert Smith.
        p. cm.
    Includes bibliographical references and index.
    ISBN-13: 978-0-325-00992-6
    ISBN-10: 0-325-00992-9
    1. Education, Bilingual—United States.   2. Immersion method (Language teaching).
I. Smith, Annette Rickert.   II. Title.   III. Title: Seven steps to success in dual language immersion.

LC3731.C3429 2006
370.117—dc22   2006019995

Editor: Lois Bridges
Production: Vicki Kasabian
Cover design: Joni Doherty Design
Typesetter: Appingo
Manufacturing: Steve Bernier

Printed in the United States of America on acid-free paper
10   09   08   07   VP   2   3   4   5

To my late father, Albert H. Rickert Jr., who shared with me a passion for the Spanish language, culture, and people. It was his belief that only through total immersion in the Spanish language would I become truly fluent. His passion for nature, people, books, and culture lives on in me, and he nurtured the values that have made my life so enjoyable and rewarding. Thank you, Daddy.

—Annette

To mi familia. Thank you for your love, patience, and support throughout my professional career, and gracias for inculcating in me a love for my heritage and language.

—Lore

Contents

Introduction

The year was 1989. Las Vegas, Nevada, was buzzing with growth and change. The nightly news, denizens of the university campus, local business executives, and dinner companions all over town were focused on one particular aspect of this dramatic transformation. A non-English-speaking labor force was pouring into an area that had no plan or infrastructure to meet the needs of English language learners (ELLs), defined by Lindholm (2000) as students who come from homes in which the family speaks a language other than English.

As the ELL student population increased, we, as classroom teachers, had been directly impacted. And so, motivated to acquire new skills and new knowledge to help us meet the needs of our students, we had each enrolled in graduate school at the University of Nevada, Las Vegas, in a newly established masters program in English as a second language (ESL). It is there we met.

Since that time, we have become the best of friends as well as coworkers, teaching, training, writing, presenting, and administrating programs with an emphasis on language acquisition. In the late nineties, we served as director (Lore) and coordinator (Annette) of second language programs in the fifth-largest school district in the nation, with an ELL student population of thirty-six thousand. During that time, our passionate concern for children whose instructional needs were not being met in traditional education led us to research the most effective programs for English language learners.

Specifically, we studied the research of Thomas and Collier (1997, 2001), who examined English language learners over a period of ten years. This longitudinal study focused on the time needed for ELLs to reach and sustain grade-level achievement in their second language, as well as on the types of programs and the instructional variables that strongly affected their long-term academic achievement. The study concluded that the most effective model for instruction was dual language education. As defined by Drs. Yvonne and David Freeman and Sandra Mercuri (2005), the label *dual language education* encapsulates the "essential component" of dual immersion, "the use of two languages for instruction." As Freeman, Freeman, and Mercuri explain, the "goal is for students to develop full conversational and academic proficiency in two languages" (xvi). As a result, we decided to investigate dual language education across the country and around the world.

Our investigation included school visits to observe students engaged in dual language instruction at various grade levels. We interviewed and consulted administrators, teachers, parents, and community leaders in Texas, Arizona, New Mexico, Illinois, Washington, Mexico, China, and Europe about the design and implementation of such programs. During these visits we also interviewed students who had achieved the goals of dual language education—students who had become bilingual (fluent in speaking two languages) and biliterate (able to read and write in two languages) and demonstrated positive cross-cultural attitudes and behavior—and we were excited by their high academic achievement. It was obvious that there were cognitive advantages to studying in two languages.

At the completion of our investigation, we were convinced that dual language programs were the most effective not just for English language learners but for all students. Our next challenge was to find the support and funding needed to change the paradigm of instruction in our school district. We applied for a Title VII federal grant (Linking Globally/Enlaces Mundiales) and obtained funding to implement the first dual language immersion program in the state of Nevada. In our application, we described a model of instruction we had developed by selecting the best instructional practices we had observed during our research: balanced literacy, integrated thematic instruction, hands-on activities, graphic organizers, and cooperative learning structures. These instructional practices and how they are used in a dual language setting are identified and explained in this book. (They can be modified to meet the needs of the school communities in which they are being implemented. Since we believe in teachers' professionalism and creativity and in the importance of personal teaching styles, we offer a model framework rather than a dictated script.) This model currently consists of a strand of two teamed (or paired) classrooms per grade level, pre-K through fifth grade, taught by partner teachers. Students switch classes in the afternoon. (More on specific organization in Step 4.)

Two Models of Dual Language Immersion

The first model funded by the grant, implemented since the fall of 2000 at Cyril Wengert Elementary School, is a 50/50 two-way dual language immersion program. Students in the program are volunteers. Half of the students are English language learners, the other half, Spanish language learners (that is, their home language is English). This model currently consists of a strand of two classrooms per grade level, pre-K through fifth grade. The students receive 50 percent of their instruction in English and 50 percent of their instruction in Spanish. (Two Chinese sisters whose home language was Mandarin also participated in the program. We had great fun teaching them, and they soon became the highest achievers of the group. By the end of the first year of instruction, the girls were speaking, reading, and writing in both Spanish and English: trilingual and triliterate. Wow!)

The second model, implemented since 2001 at J. Marlan Walker International School, is a 50/50 one-way dual language immersion program. The first year the school opened, all but three of the kindergartners who participated in the program were Spanish language learners. They received 50 percent of their instruction in English and 50 percent of their instruction in Spanish. Every year an additional grade level has been added. Currently there are more than 1,100 students in the program, which provides a challenging and enriching curriculum.

(Since the inception of the aforementioned programs, five other schools located in the Clark County school district have also implemented dual language immersion programs.)

About This Book

This book is divided into seven steps for implementing a dual language immersion program. A concluding chapter describes an international dual language immersion school.

Step 1, "Understanding and Planning for Dual Language Immersion," provides the theoretical framework for these programs. It also describes instructional strategies that focus on language acquisition and literacy skill. You can create transparencies and/or handouts for staff development training with the numbered and bulleted outlines found in this chapter.

Step 2, "Organizing the Classroom," identifies the five essential components of a properly prepared environment: physical arrangement, established rituals, peace and serenity, freedom with responsibility, and classroom awareness. Teachers' biggest challenge and most laborious task is preparing their classroom for student-directed learning. This entails arranging furniture and content-area centers so that students, in manipulating their environment, will build both gross and fine motor skills. Students need to be able and encouraged to move freely and safely about the classroom if they are to become responsible, independent learners.

Students become confident and feel secure in an environment of consistent rituals and procedures. They know what is expected of them and become socially successful. Another important consistency that supports students and their success in acquiring bilingualism and biliteracy is mirrored classrooms: the classrooms of the dual language teachers use the same rituals and procedures and have similar furniture arrangements and center activities.

Step 3, "Planning Instruction," emphasizes the importance of the collaborative effort between partner teachers and the sharing of thematic units among grade-level teachers. Thematic units are based on science and social studies topics determined by grade-level standards and unique to the grade level. These theme units, which are stored in large bins, include big books, lesson plans, trade books, concrete center activities, and a variety of supplemental materials. Content areas of reading, writing, and arithmetic are integrated within the theme units.

The theme topic is supported in each partner teacher's classroom in similar ways to promote a natural development of concepts and vocabulary. Teachers activate prior knowledge through the use of graphic organizers in class discussion and draw interest from students with visuals and real objects.

Partner teachers plan a theme unit together using a two-page web organizer. Sharing the responsibility of planning reduces stress, especially for teachers new to the program. Thorough planning includes brainstorming ideas and predetermining weaknesses before instruction begins. Joint planning is essential for successful teaching.

Step 4, "Teaching Through Best Practice," looks at a day in a dual language immersion classroom. It describes both morning and afternoon primary and intermediate schedules and details academic instruction. It also addresses necessary instructional strategies for language acquisition. Dual language teachers develop lessons with two objectives in mind. The first is based on concept development, the second, language acquisition. Teachers of second language learners need to provide lessons in a low-risk environment and scaffold their instruction with graphic organizers, academic word walls, visuals, and concrete materials to ensure student understanding.

Step 5, "Learning Through Hands-On Activities," emphasizes the importance of hands-on activities as a means to engage students in learning and support the goal of a student-directed classroom. These interactive activities make abstract concepts clear and concrete. Children become independent workers who are developing an internal sense of worth, self-discipline, and a lifetime work ethic.

In using these activities, students make personal choices as well as explore and investigate their interests. Each activity is purposeful and is tied to grade-level standards and appropriate time lines. Activities must be displayed in an orderly, appealing manner (a basket or tray is recommended) and include everything necessary to complete the activity. Some type of boundary cloth is usually included to define the students' work space.

Respectful movement around the classroom and the cautious transporting of materials builds both gross and fine motor skills. Additionally, children learn to move in space gracefully without spills or damage and acquire respect for the boundaries of other people. When students work independently, with peers, or in small groups at center activities, the teacher has the freedom to observe, record, assess, and redirect their learning. In third through fifth grade, centers become process based in order to stimulate higher-order thinking skills: students invent, research, investigate, and explore, and teachers expect students to be able to justify, defend, and debate their results.

Step 6, "Assessing as a Way to Better Instruction and Accountability," explores a variety of assessment tools that facilitate data-driven instruction. Current federal accountability has necessitated an increased focus on individual student progress. Teachers must accommodate every student, recognizing individual learning styles and whatever special considerations are required. An accurate analysis of student knowledge also requires a variety of authentic assessments. By observing students, teachers become aware of each individual student's ability to problem solve, accomplish goals, and master learning objectives.

Norm-referenced assessments are required by individual states and allow the test scores of immersion education students to be compared with their peers across the nation. Criterion-referenced assessments give teachers the data they need to plan their instruction. Authentic assessments give students alternative ways to demonstrate what they know when traditional tests do not.

Step 7, "Building Community Support," addresses the needs of the current business community, gives suggestions on how to secure the support of this community, and offers examples of how to seek out positive media coverage and contact local businesses. This step also reinforces the critical role parents play in maintaining immersion programs and offers suggestions for educating parents about such a program; describes the kind of leadership needed to ensure the program is successful; and itemizes the characteristics of immersion teachers and the attributes of students educated in a dual language immersion school.

The book's conclusion describes the J. Marlan Walker International School and its curriculum concentrating on language, geography, global concepts, academic achievement, information analysis, communication skills, citizenship, technology, and career preparation. It emphasizes how important it is for students to gain bilingual and bicultural competence, therefore allowing them to become successful participants in the global community and economy.

Why Dual Language Immersion? (Or, Better, Why Not?)

When Annette was fifteen, her father enrolled her in boarding school, Santa Maria del Camino, in Puerta de Hierro, Madrid, Spain. Attendance at this unique international school was a world-class educational opportunity. It was there she fell in love with learning and then with sharing what she learned with others. The teachers at Santa Maria del Camino used many of the instructional methods advocated in this book. They modeled a love of learning Annette found to be contagious. Through the experiences these teachers provided, the students absorbed knowledge. They were taken to museums, historical monuments, plays, concerts, operas, factories, markets, courts, government buildings, and so on. Anthropologists, scientists, architects, artists, and dancers conducted seminars. Students performed regularly in dance and musical concerts, theatre performances, and sports events. They investigated, experimented, discussed, debated, cooked, sewed, knitted, and painted. Excursions to the mountains, the seacoasts, the plains, and the forest stimulated the senses. Through this natural approach to learning, Annette became bilingual, biliterate, and bicultural. She also realized she would be a teacher.

Why not provide these experiences to every child? Why not provide this kind of education for free in public education? It can be done. Especially now, with the virtual opportunities available through technology, students can experience the world even if confined within the walls of the school building.

There is an immediate need for an education that prepares students to be able to take a global perspective. Thankfully, dual language immersion programs are gaining momentum throughout the United States as an exemplary means of educating all students and enriching their educational experience. Through dual language programs, students not only become proficient in two languages but also develop an understanding of and appreciation for the cultures associated with the languages—and very often in the process demonstrate high achievement in all core academic subjects (Cloud, Genesee, and Hamayan 2000). The doubts and stresses of the general public caused by the paradigm shift from traditional education to dual language immersion are typically relieved by the success dual language immersion students and teachers both experience.

Our own passionate quest has taken us on an exciting journey. We have enjoyed traveling, interviewing other experts, and teaching in dual language programs, but above all we have enjoyed seeing our students become fluent and literate in more than one language. We invite you to journey with us through the seven steps to a successful dual language immersion program. Turn the page and join us.

7 Steps to Success in Dual Language Immersion

Step 1

Understanding and Planning
for Dual Language Immersion

*The task of a modern educator is not to cut down jungles, but
to irrigate deserts.*

—C. S. Lewis

Journal Entry
November 2, 2005

I am feeling so empowered and on top of things, I've been teaching for eight years
now and recognize that this is a career that always challenges. I never feel as if I can
sit back on my laurels and coast along because there is always an excitement of learning, improving, preparing, and staying ahead of my students in order to challenge
them. I thought that everything would be planned and in place after the first year, and
then I could just repeat my plans from year to year, instead I find that I am never sat-
isfied with those basic plans. I have an inner urge to grow, learn and improve. Every
year I learn more through training and personal experience and every year I have a
different group of students with their own set of needs. I love that I have learned to
differentiate my instruction through dual language training. I cannot imagine teaching any other way. My partner and I together plan for growth in each child. There are
two of us to observe and identify special needs of individual students. Together we discuss how to meet those needs. Sometimes she shocks me with her brilliant ideas and
she compliments me as well so I guess two brains are better than one.

—*Second-Grade Teacher*

The most important aspect of any dual language immersion program is professional development and planning. Obviously, implementing this program requires
a drastic paradigm shift in teaching, and much preparation and planning needs to
be in place before a school begins to implement the program. In our particular situation, we were awarded a financial opportunity through grant funding to put our
seven-step model into practice. As a result we did our planning and preparation

simultaneously during our first year of implementation. That experience proved to be overwhelming, and we do not recommend it to others if you wish to have a life beyond school.

Now when we assist a school with implementation, we recommend a year of planning, preparing, and of course training. In this year of preparation, units are developed, shelf activities are created, materials are ordered, parent awareness and support are provided through informational meetings, and the seven steps are modeled and further developed through professional training. This will simplify the first year of the program and facilitate a positive experience for everyone involved. It is important to celebrate the small steps and successes in order to excite participants to meet the academic challenges of developing bilingualism and biliteracy and foster in students a global awareness.

An essential element in administrative planning is to structure a schedule that provides mutual planning time for partner teachers as often as possible. The best scenario would be daily mutual preparation periods for partner teachers and weekly grade-level team meetings to plan the sharing of materials, ideas, and units.

Maintaining high standards requires that teachers receive bilingual and/or English as a second language certification (Montague 1997). Comprehensive dual language professional development includes training in second language acquisition, journaling, the writing process, balanced literacy, graphic organizers, process-based activities, math methods, cultural enrichment, cooperative learning, and alternative assessment. With skills like these, teachers can become peer coaches and strategists at their schools, and the students benefit from appropriate instruction. To get you started, here is an overview of dual language education theory, language acquisition theory and methods, and balanced literacy strategies.

The Sociocultural Theory Behind Dual Language Education

The sociocultural advantages of knowing more than one language include a greater intercultural understanding and tolerance as well as an appreciation and respect for cultural differences (Cloud, Genesee, and Hamayan 2000). Language cannot be isolated from the sociocultural context of the classroom or the larger world. Vygotsky (1986) holds that higher levels of cognition are both formed and expressed through language, which is developed in social processes (Wink and Putney 2002). At the core of Vygotsky's theory is the influence of social processes on higher mental functions and the development of these cognitive capacities, which are social in origin and mediated by changing uses of language (Wertsch 1985).

In Vygotskian theory, the learner must receive assistance by way of social interaction with significant others before he can ascertain meaning; the learner then reconceptualizes the learning into a novel form of understanding and knowledge based on prior and present experiences, thus gaining a new way of responding to and solving problems that is similar but not identical to those used by the teacher (Diaz, Neal, and Amaya-Williams 1990). The teacher initially regulates the learning activity in order to create a level of intersubjectivity. Vygotsky (1978) refers to this social process as moving from other-regulated to self-regulated learning. Other-regulated learning enables learners to converse about and perform tasks that are beyond their individual capability at the time the tasks are introduced. Self-regulation means the learner is able to plan, guide, and monitor problem-solving activities similar to those performed jointly without adult assistance (Diaz, Neal, and Amaya-Williams 1990).

Vygotsky identifies the difference between actual and potential levels of learning as the *zone of proximal development*. This social learning principle is a function of both the learner's level of development and the nature of the instruction being given. Teachers are working within students' zones of proximal development when they help learners participate in the lesson from the very beginning. As learners gain conceptual understanding through discussion and practice, the boundaries of the zone gradually expand into new areas of knowledge, in terms of both what can be done independently and what can be done with assistance (Faltis 1997).

Attitudes and policies regarding the language education program and its participants can positively or negatively influence a program's outcomes (Troike 1978). If community, administration, and staff attitudes toward bilingualism and language minority students are favorable, language education policies are more likely to result in high-quality programs and high levels of literacy and academic achievement (Willig 1985). When attitudes are negative, it is unlikely language education programs will be implemented unless they are mandatory, and they will tend to result in lower levels of academic achievement and language proficiency (Lindholm 1992).

As Linney and Seidman (1989) point out in their review of the literature on how schools and teachers affect student outcomes, the quality of a child's school experience is important not only for academic achievement but also for fostering self-esteem, self-confidence, and general psychological well-being. Teachers tend to expect less of lower-class ethnic minority students and expect more of middle-class white students (Dusek 1985), which results in differential treatment, which results in differential outcomes (Brophy 1986). Student interactions within the classroom also have an impact on student achievement.

Allport (1954) proposes four core conditions that will improve intergroup relations and maximize the achievement of all students:

1. Assign equal status to minority and majority students.
2. Have students work interdependently on tasks with common objectives.
3. Give students the opportunity to interact with one another as individuals.
4. Support student-to-student contact.

Research demonstrates unequivocal support for cooperative learning in achieving better ethnic relations and more self-esteem (Slavin 1983). When students work in ethnically mixed cooperative learning groups, their friendships cross ethnic boundaries. Dual language education is built on providing language learners with the most positive social context in which to develop bilingual competence. Both linguistic minority and majority students benefit from a social context in which all languages and cultures are equally valued and all students are treated equally. More specifically, integrating native English speakers and native speakers of another language facilitates second language acquisition because it promotes authentic, meaningful interaction among speakers of the two languages (Genesee 1987).

Theory and Methods of Language Acquisition

Genesee's (1987) long-term research on language acquisition has shown that individuals who begin second language learning early are more likely than those who begin later to achieve nativelike levels of proficiency. Here are some other documented findings:

1. Considerable language learning occurs naturally during non–language arts classes like math or social studies in which children communicate with each other about non-language-related issues (Genesee 1984).

2. The second language learner progresses according to her own rate and style in much the same way that first language learners do (Genesee 1984).

3. Early immersion in a second language takes advantage of children's special metalinguistic, psycholinguistic, and cognitive capacities to learn language (Genesee 1984; Lambert 1984).

4. Language used with students needs to be adjusted to their conceptual and linguistic levels.

5. Concentrated exposure to language is important to promote language development.

6. The two languages are kept distant and never mixed during instruction. For example, in an English-Spanish dual language program, two teachers are responsible for instructing a group of students. Both teachers are considered pure language models. The English-speaking teacher instructs only in English and the Spanish-speaking teacher instructs only in Spanish.

In a classic study, Peal and Lambert (1962) found that exposure to both languages gave French-English bilinguals an advantage. Their experiences with two languages resulted in mental flexibility, better conceptualization, and more diversified mental abilities. In contrast, the monolinguals' unitary cognition restricted their verbal problem-solving ability. Furthermore, Cummins (1987) proposed the common underlying proficiency theory, which posits that developing knowledge and proficiency in one language facilitates learning in the second language. A bilingual who performs well in math in one language is very likely to perform well in math in a second language, even after only one or two years of schooling in the second language, once the student is proficient enough in the language to demonstrate that knowledge (Lindholm 1992).

Researchers have also found that two-way dual language programs are more effective in developing first and second language academic achievement. The findings of the Ramirez report (Cummins 1992) indicate Latino students who receive sustained primary language instruction throughout elementary school have better academic prospects than those who receive most or all of their instruction in English. Ramirez emphasizes three central psychoeducational principles, which also underlie enrichment bilingual education programs:

1. The continued development of two languages enhances children's educational and cognitive development.

2. Literacy-related knowledge and skills acquired in one language are potentially available in another language.

3. While second language conversational abilities may be acquired fairly rapidly, it usually takes five or more years for second language learners to attain grade norms in academically related aspects of the second language.

Together, these principles suggest that reinforcing children's first language throughout elementary school and beyond provides a foundation for long-term growth in English academic skills (Cummins 1992).

Thomas and Collier (1997), investigating school services provided to language minority students in five large urban and suburban school districts in various parts of the United States, examined and interpreted more than seven hundred thousand student records. They statistically determined the length of time it would take non-English-proficient students to reach the fiftieth NCE (normal curve equivalent) on a standardized English reading subtest administered in English both with and without instruction in the student's primary language. They also compared achievement (in NCEs) on standardized tests in English reading for six types of second language instructional programs. Language minority students in bilingual programs scored higher than students in English as a second language programs, and students in two-way bilingual programs scored highest of all. This study generated three key findings:

1. Academic knowledge acquired via one language paves the way for the acquisition of related knowledge and skills in another language.
2. English is best acquired after a child's first language is firmly established. Specifically, strong oral and literacy skills developed in a first language provide a solid base for the acquisition of literacy and other academic language skills in English (Edelsky 1982).
3. Immersion programs for language majority students enable them to develop advanced levels of second language proficiency without compromising their academic achievement or first language development (Genesee 1984).

These findings suggest that a key predictor of academic success is receiving cognitively complex at-grade-level academic instruction in students' first language at least through grade 5 or 6.

Here are some other important observations:

- Language acquisition is long term and occurs naturally during childhood. Caretakers offer positive feedback and encouragement, and children become fluent speakers in five or six years.
- Language acquisition is facilitated through hands-on activities and visuals that support comprehension.

- Language is learned best in nonstressful environments in which students can interact socially and academically and are encouraged to make use of the second language.
- Students are motivated to acquire their second language because they need to use it to function in their school environment.

Appendix A lists the stages of language acquisition along with typical student behavior at each stage and instructional approaches relative to each stage. Appendix B lists general instructional strategies that facilitate language acquisition.

Sheltered Instruction

Sheltered instruction provides students with additional support to enhance their understanding of concepts being presented during the lesson. Teachers carefully select materials, resources, and instructional strategies that will allow all students to access grade-level, content-related curriculum. They

- determine the text to be sheltered
- rewrite the text, focusing on the essential concepts and presenting them in a simplified way
- teach using this sheltered text and any supplemental materials available to support meaning.

Following are the steps in a sheltered lesson:

1. *Day 1*: Activate prior knowledge as a class or in cooperative groups. Graphic organizers such as a K-W-L chart (what you *know*, what you *want* to know, what you *learned*) are effective tools students can use to brainstorm ideas related to the topic being studied.
2. *Day 2*: Read the sheltered text as a class, in small groups, or individually. Ask students to highlight the important sentences in the text. Have each student select a sentence, rewrite it, and illustrate the meaning. Sequence these illustrated pages to form a class book.
3. *Day 3*: Build excitement and interest by providing visuals, realia, guest speakers, videos, and experiments that support the meaning of the text.
4. *Day 4*: Have students, in cooperative groups, review the text and record what they know about it on chart paper. Every member of the group writes a sentence. They edit each other's sentences for accuracy, display their charts, and finally report their findings to the whole class.
5. *Day 5*: Assess students' knowledge of the sheltered text. (Use a variety of assessments, depending on the students' language proficiency.)

Total Physical Response

Traditional second language teaching uses left-brain strategies such as "listen and repeat after me," "memorize this dialogue," "learn this vocabulary list," and "pronounce these words." Total physical response (TPR) instruction is based on the way infants acquire a first language, through physical interaction. It prompts the right side of the brain to retain knowledge using images, music, and spatial concepts.

In the home, language is acquired naturally through interactions among family members. Infants initially respond with physical actions and are not required to speak. Parents and family members then begin to encourage one- or two-word utterances. Nonverbal responses or yes-or-no answers are also accepted. In a language acquisition classroom, the teacher needs to replicate this home environment, which is not stressful and is highly motivating. A period of silence, varying with the individual, should be expected as students begin to comprehend their second language. Students begin by using one or two words, often switching between their native and second languages. Teachers accept students' grammatical errors in their second language and model the correct forms.

Journals

Three types of journals often figure in dual language immersion. *Daily journaling* in the primary grades is described in Step 4. In their staff development teachers should experience journaling themselves through the typical five-step process (thinking, drawing, telling, writing, and reading) as the staff developer models and verbalizes each step. Practicing journaling in small groups allows them to implement this five-step process comfortably in their own classroom.

Dialogue, or interactive, journals in the intermediate grades are also discussed in Step 4. A staff developer should give teachers a variety of prompts or options to write about. Then, with a partner or in small groups, teachers can respond to each other's writing. These responses should focus on voice and creativity rather than on syntactic structure.

Content-based journals are used throughout the grade levels as a way for students taking part in a hands-on activity or an investigative process to record their thoughts and newly acquired knowledge. These journals give students an opportunity to move from concrete experiences to abstract thoughts; the teacher can use them as a basis for assessment; and they enhance students' listening, speaking, reading, and writing skills. Also, a note-taking habit like this will serve students well in higher education when they must identify and extract important elements of a lecture or passage, analyze and apply that information, and then reciprocate with their own interpretation.

Students answer three questions in their content-based journals, which challenge them to develop their critical-thinking skills:

1. What activity are you doing?
2. How are you doing this activity?
3. What did you learn from this activity?

A staff developer should introduce content-based journals in connection with a process-based activity. Teachers need time to practice what their students will be required to perform.

The Writing Process

Teachers should understand the recursive nature of the writing process and have some sense of the various phases of writing; typically writers cycle through the following stages:

1. prewriting
   - generating ideas
   - conceptualizing thoughts
   - activating prior knowledge
2. drafting
   - determining purpose
   - putting ideas on paper
3. revising
   - researching
   - problem solving
   - organizing
4. editing
   - clarifying
   - refining
5. publishing
   - presenting the piece to a selected audience

Many school district professional development centers and university teacher education programs offer courses in the writing process; additionally, teachers will find an array of excellent professional resources including *Writing Workshop: The Essential Guide* (Fletcher and Portalupi 2001) and *Writing Essentials: Raising Expectations and Results While Simplifying Teaching* (Routman 2005).

Educators implementing this process as a component of their program should have the benefit of having undertaken a major writing project of their own. After we finished the first draft of this book, we celebrated with champagne, joyous exclamations of completion, and dancing in the school halls, only to be reminded by our editor that we were still in the early stages of the process. After many years of nagging our students to view writing as a five-step process, how quickly we'd forgotten!

In training teachers to use dual language immersion programs, the staff developer needs to provide opportunities for the teachers to work in small groups so they'll develop the necessary skill and confidence for teaching. Acceptance and encouragement from a small group expands writers' courage and dissipates their fears, inhibitions, and aversions.

Reading-Writing Workshop

In a reading-writing workshop the teacher devotes extended periods of time to students' uninterrupted literacy development. These long intervals integrate reading, writing, and research across the curriculum. Instruction in social studies, science, and math is integrated in thematic units that incorporate fiction and nonfiction from a variety of genres. Here's the general breakdown:

Whole-Group Instruction (ten- or fifteen-minute minilesson)
- Teacher focuses on a state standard literacy objective.

Independent, Paired, and Small-Group Work (forty to sixty minutes)
- Students read independently, with a partner, or in literacy circles.
- Activities include silent sustained reading, book reviews, projects, small-group shares and literature discussions, response journals, and individual conferences.

Whole-Group Connections (fifteen to twenty minutes)
- Class discusses and shares thoughts and insights.

Individual Connections (fifteen to twenty minutes)
- Each student writes connections in a response journal.

Balanced Literacy Strategies

Reading cannot be confined to one period of the day: it is part of any exchange of meaning via text. What children acquire during focused reading instruction impacts all learning. Reading is the key to academic success. Therefore, reading instruction is integrated throughout all curricular subjects. In balanced literacy the teacher makes informal decisions about the learning opportunities offered to children so that they will find reading an enjoyable and successful experience.

Balanced literacy experiences include modeled reading and writing, shared reading and writing, guided reading and writing, independent reading and writing, language exploration, language experience, partner reading, and skill and strategy instruction. The best learning opportunities incorporate flexible groupings—heterogeneous for whole-group instruction, homogeneous for small-group instruction—to accommodate individual needs.

Children learn to read by being surrounded by talk and print. The teacher has the privilege of developing a child's love of reading by selecting interesting texts, making connections with children's prior experiences, showing the children how to think as they read, constructing meaning with children, and demonstrating reading strategies. Reading is an ongoing process of evolved thinking. When readers read, they carry on an inner conversation with the text. It is essential for students to recognize how important their thinking is when they read. It's our job as teachers to convince students that their thoughts, ideas, and interpretations matter. When readers engage in the text and listen to their inner conversation, they enhance their understanding, build knowledge, and develop insight (Harvey and Goudvis 2000).

Figure 1–1 shows the instructional components of balanced literacy. In a balanced literacy approach, graphophonic elements (those having to do with sounds, symbols, and analogies) and print conventions (directionality, words and spaces, letters, beginnings and endings, and punctuation) are taught within a meaningful context rather than in isolation.

In the past, literacy instruction began with the smallest pieces, individual letters and sounds, then syllables, words, phrases, sentences, paragraphs, and finally whole texts. This proved successful with some students. Then the pendulum swung to the complete opposite; literacy instruction began with the whole text and moved to the smallest parts. This also proved successful with some students.

Currently a more balanced literacy approach is used in which teachers begin with the whole text, move to selected parts for specific purposes, and then go back to the whole text. Teachers pull meaningful samples from the text to teach specific skills, such as letter identification, patterns, decoding strategies, onsets and rimes, and word recognition. Students expand these skills by applying what they have learned through rereading, rewriting, responding, dialoguing, and role-playing. This balanced approach considers the learning needs of all students.

Read-Alouds

Reading aloud, or modeled reading, provides students with a good example of reading fluency. The teacher enunciates clearly, uses an appropriate speech rate, reads with expression, and in general serves as a model reader worthy of imitation. All students benefit from listening to stories, poems, and informational text read aloud. They acquire information from text that is too hard for them to have read on their own. It is important for the teacher to select a text the students will find interesting.

Shared Reading

Shared reading is discussed in Step 4. It is a valuable technique to use with beginning readers because it models the process of reading and allows students to

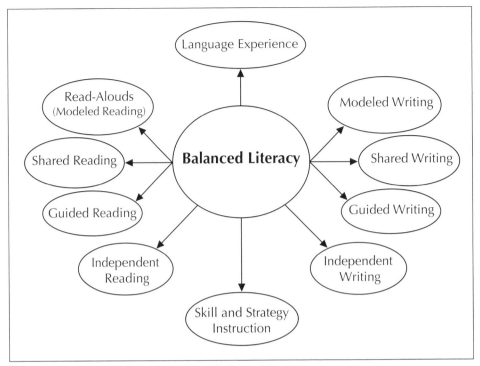

Figure 1–1. Structural Components of Balanced Literacy

participate actively. A text selected for shared reading should include familiar language, patterned structures, and a predictable plot. First the teacher discusses the familiar language via a picture walk or a graphic organizer to activate prior knowledge and set the stage for learning appropriate to the students' language proficiency. Students in the preproduction stage of language acquisition can participate via total physical response (drawing and pantomiming, for example). Students in the early production stage can participate using these same types of physical responses and also by responding to yes-or-no questions, either-or questions, or referential questions (*who, what, when, where*). Picture walks can include simple repetitive chants. Speech-emergent students, working in pairs or in collaborative groups, can participate in the aforementioned activities as well as make predictions about the text (sequence pictures from the text in order to predict the story, for example). Students who are somewhat more fluent can participate in all of the previous activities and work in collaborative teams with graphic organizers.

After the teacher has read a text aloud, the class or group reads it together using a shared source—from a big book, on the overhead projector, or on a chart.

Texts usually have elements of rhythm and repetition and are reread many times. Teachers unlock the meaning of the text through discussion.

Shared reading can be broken down into these six steps:

1. Before reading the text, the teacher
   - checks for prior knowledge
   - builds background and vocabulary
2. The teacher introduces the text. He
   - discusses parts of the book
   - introduces author and illustrator
   - supports the text with manipulatives and visuals
   - conducts a picture walk to encourage predictions
3. The teacher reads to the children. He
   - reads the story aloud with enthusiasm
   - pauses to answer questions and verify predictions
   - makes the story an enjoyable experience
   - uses illustrations to facilitate comprehension
   - tracks words with a pointer
   - models expression
   - talks in character
   - exaggerates expression to support comprehension
4. The teacher reads with the children. He
   - controls the rate of reading fluency
   - enunciates clearly
   - encourages participation
   - checks for comprehension
   - stimulates discussion by questioning students:
     Favorite part?
     Funniest part?
     Character reminds you of . . .
5. The teacher and students reread sections to model strategies:
   - predicting
   - finding patterns
   - sequencing
   - comparing and contrasting
   - integrating the three cueing systems (semantic, syntactic, graphophonic)
6. The students read the text, engaging in
   - text-to-picture activities
   - storyboarding

- personal response drawings
- participation through gestures, sound effects, and movement

Extension Activities
- book rewrites
- story dramatizations
- book responses
- collaborative class books
- text illustrations

Guided Reading

Guided reading is described in Step 4. It is an enabling, empowering approach to literacy instruction based on the understanding that children bring meaning to and gain meaning from the text as they read. The aim of guided reading is to develop independent readers who question, consider alternatives, and make informed choices as they seek meaning. While reading, students explore and discover themselves and their world through the author's message. For guided reading instruction, the teacher groups four, five, or six children of similar reading ability for a fifteen- to twenty-minute lesson. These groups are flexible and temporary. The teacher selects a text that offers a manageable number of challenges for the students in the group and helps children acquire new skills to meet these challenges.

The focus of guided reading is on modeling and using strategies for understanding and discussing the text. The teacher creates a low-stress environment, which promotes confidence and security. Reading a comfortable text in a small group enhances reading fluency. Here's a breakdown of the steps and strategies:

Before Guided Reading
- Determine students' guided reading level.
- Group students according to reading fluency.
- Select a running record assessment.
- Choose a leveled book for each guided reading group.
- Arrange an appropriate classroom area for guided reading.
- Prepare shelf activities and train students to work on their own to ensure all students are working purposefully.

Introducing the Text
- Reread previous text.
- Discuss parts of the new text.
- Clarify difficult vocabulary.
- Acknowledge cognates.

- Activate prior knowledge.
- Discuss the genre and purpose of the text.
- Make predictions about the text.

First Reading of the Text

- Model reading the text with expression and intonation.
- Have students whisper read the text together.
- Ask students to track the words in the text as they read.
- Focus students on the visuals to construct meaning.
- Monitor and support students as they read.
- Discuss characters, plot, events, and illustrations.
- Model reading strategies.

Teaching Reading Skills Through the Text

- concepts of print
- difficult vocabulary
- words known on sight
- grammar
- comprehension
- graphophonics
- phonological awareness
- extracting meaning from the text
- decoding skills
- author's purpose

Language Experience

The language experience approach to writing helps students connect oral and written language. It is a powerful tool by which teachers model using language correctly. A concrete group experience involving objects students can manipulate becomes the stimulus for the story. As students take turns dictating the story, the teacher accepts what they say, repeats it using correct grammar and sentence structure, and records the quote (with correct spelling) on chart paper or a transparency. Then the class reads the text together chorally as the teacher tracks the words with a pointer, showing left-to-right and top-to-bottom directionality. These stories can be copied to create individual and/or class books for students to reread as a group, with partners, or independently.

This exercise is especially beneficial to students acquiring a second language because all students can participate in the experience. Students who can't yet produce language can listen as more proficient students dictate. Comprehension is aided by the concrete experience they have previously shared. Students at a very early stage of language proficiency can chant predictable patterns or parts along with the group.

Students who are just starting to be able to speak can contribute to the story with the aid of a graphic organizer. Students who are more fluent can read and copy the text.

Comprehension

Reading comprehension is about much more than answering literal questions at the end of a passage, story, or chapter. Reading comprehension is an ongoing process of evolved thinking. When readers read, they carry on an inner conversation with the text: they respond with delight, wonder, even outrage. They question the text, argue with the author, and nod their head in agreement. They make connections, ask questions, and draw inferences to better understand and learn from what they read (Harvey and Goudvis 2000).

Keene and Zimmermann (1997) identify three connections the reader makes while reading. The first is a text-to-self connection, in which the reader reflects on her own life in order to build a more relevant relationship with the text. The second is a text-to-text connection, in which the reader is reminded of other texts she has read. This connection can stimulate higher-level thinking through comparison and contrast. The purpose is to help the reader understand a text more effectively. What the reader already knows will change because of what she has read. The third is a text-to-world connection, in which the reader approaches the text through the eyes of others. When the reader makes a text-to-world connection, she reflects on prior knowledge and broadens her perspective. What the reader knows may change because of what she has read.

A teacher can share the metacognitive processes that occur while reading by thinking aloud in order to comprehend the text. The teacher articulates the strategies an experienced reader uses in order to read with comprehension, selecting a challenging passage containing some unknown words and stopping to think aloud, thus modeling the thought processes involved in solving those words. The teacher then invites students to share their thoughts.

Vocabulary Study

Vocabulary is a predictor of reading fluency and comprehension. In dual language immersion programs, classrooms display vocabulary on two word walls, one a bank of high-frequency words, the other vocabulary related to the content areas (supported by visual representations of the words' meaning). Word wall activities (adapted from Cunningham 1995) provide repeated exposure to these words and promote automatic word recognition and comprehension:

1. *Word sorts:* Words are sorted in a variety of ways:
    *   first (or last, or second) letter, etc.
    *   vowel sound (short *a*, long *a*, etc.)

- spelling pattern (double consonants, etc.)
- rime pattern (*ear, ight, ar,* etc.)
- silent letters
- categories (living things, adverbs, solids, etc.)

2. *Guess the Word:* The teacher thinks of a word on the wall and gives clues. The students write down a guess after each clue is given. For example:

   Clue 1: I'm thinking of a word with five letters.

   Clue 2: It has two vowels.

   Clue 3: One of the vowels is silent.

   Clue 4: It begins with a *t.*

3. *Find a Rhyme:* The teacher tells the children to find the word that starts with a certain letter and rhymes with a word beginning with another letter. For example, "Find a word that begins with *b* and rhymes with *toy.*"

4. *Which Word Fits?* Students must decide which wall word beginning with a given letter makes sense in a sentence. For example, "Find a word that starts with *f* and fits in this sentence: I like to play with my _____."

5. *Bingo:* Children select wall words and write them on a bingo-type grid. The teacher reads off words at random. Children chant the spelling of each word and then cover it with a marker if it appears on their grid. The first student to complete a row wins the game.

6. *Word Search:* The teacher asks the students to find all of the wall words that have a particular feature. For example, "Find all of the words with *an* in them" (*can, and, want, Anthony, clean*).

Reading Simultaneously

According to Freeman, Freeman, and Mercuri (2005), if, in fact, written language can be acquired in the same way as oral language, then students can be expected to learn to read in two languages simultaneously in the same way that children brought up in bilingual households develop the ability to speak and understand two or more languages at the same time. As long as teachers make the written input comprehensible, students should be able to acquire the ability to read and write two or more languages at once.

Balanced dual language immersion programs teach initial literacy naturally, instead of by emphasizing decoding skills; they provide scaffolds for comprehension. In early literacy, teachers select leveled books that provide the readers with illustrations that support understanding. Oral language and written language are developed simultaneously in both languages of instruction through the use of thematic units, mirrored classrooms, interactive collaboration, sensorial shelf activities, and a print-rich environment. Teachers use illustrations, drama, role-playing, and concrete objects to make language comprehensible. By using the previously described best practices for language acquisition and making a commitment to high academic achievement, teachers will create proficient biliterate readers. Hudelson's (1984) research supports the idea that in dual language programs students can learn to read and write in both languages at once even if they are not proficient in both orally. She concludes, "The processes of writing, reading, speaking, and listening in a second language are interrelated and interdependent" (237).

Concepts developed in the child's first language (L1) do not need to be retaught in the child's second language (L2). For example, when a student learns in L1 that sentences begin with a capital letter, there is no need to reteach that concept in L2. The strategy of using context clues to determine the meaning of an unknown word is also accessible regardless of the language in which a student is reading. It is essential that partner teachers plan collaboratively to support the concept development occurring in each other's classroom by reteaching, practicing, and encouraging higher-level thinking.

In a dual language immersion program, the L1 pure language teacher and the L2 pure language teacher plan their balanced literacy instruction using similar methods. This facilitates the transfer of skills. Their focus is on the similarities of the languages rather than the differences. As an example, in a Spanish-English dual language program, they place emphasis on cognates such as *museum* and *museo*, *art* and *arte*, and *telephone* and *teléfono*. There are many similarities in the graphophonic, syntactic, and semantic structures of the English and Spanish languages. In effective reading programs, teachers keep students focused on meaning as they read and write in their first and second languages. Teachers know that literacy knowledge and skills developed in one language will transfer to a second language as long as the similarities between the languages are emphasized and the instructional methods are consistent (Freeman, Freeman, and Mercuri 2005).

Summary

A dual language immersion program will be only as good as the teachers. These teachers must love their students enough to set high goals and provide whatever it takes for students to reach those goals. Additionally, the teachers must be given training in research-based instructional best practice. They need time to implement and opportunities to build working relationships with partner teachers and grade-level teams. Collaborative grade-level teams that share and support one another benefit everyone. Teachers and others involved in the implementation of dual language immersion programs must also focus their efforts on gaining community support. In the next step, we explain how to organize the classroom environment.

Organizing the Classroom

I never teach my pupils; I only attempt to provide the conditions in which they can learn.

—Albert Einstein

Journal Entry
October 14, 2005

It is amazing how I've been able to train our students to maintain our learning space. They did not come to me with these skills! Most new students entering the program are used to leaving clean up to the custodians and messes to the teacher. Quickly they learn that is not the case here. They meet our expectations and taking care of themselves and their environment builds their self-esteem. If I did it myself I am sure I would get resentful, grumpy, and work through the night. If my classroom was run in the teacher-directed fashion of the past I feel my career would be short lived due to burn out. How could one person meet the needs of so many students all day long, day after day. My students live and learn in a self-directed, independent learning classroom environment. I see my job to be the preparer of the environment and the facilitator of instruction.

—*Third-Grade Teacher*

The first step in dual language immersion is preparing a classroom that is beautiful, inviting, and peaceful and that motivates children to love learning as a way of life. This environment is clean, simple, and organized. Students' attention is narrowed to the task at hand through the elimination of clutter and overstimulation. Children today have busy lives bombarded with sensory messages: television, radios, billboards, street noise, computer games, and the Internet. Their classrooms need to be a haven of tranquility, a place in which they can focus. Soft classical music playing in the background helps create a peaceful classroom.

Students also need the freedom to move and the opportunity to choose their personal work spaces. To accomplish this without chaos requires detailed, thorough training during the first few weeks of school. Students need to learn to move and carry materials while always respecting the space and property of others. For example, they should carry chairs with their right hand on the top back and their left hand on the seat bottom, chair legs pointed to the floor. They should hold activity trays with two steady hands, focusing on arriving at their destination without accidents. They should select work locations that are out of the flow of traffic. Basically, the classroom arrangement must allow all of its occupants to work together efficiently and respectfully.

Teachers also need to give a lot of thought and consideration to the rituals that will foster intellectual growth, inner discipline, and peace in the children they teach and provide predictability and order in children's lives. Consistent procedures and schedules give students a sense of security and ownership. A child who is proud of his accomplishments and has a sense of belonging will grow up strong and secure. Once teachers have prepared the classroom, trained students in its ways of operation, and established their expectations, their job becomes much easier.

In kindergarten, the environment is enriched by including practical life skills such as setting the table, dressing, washing one's hands, folding towels, cleaning, sweeping, polishing, gardening, and organizing. Students develop their fine and gross motor skills, as well as courteous manners, by walking and carrying things carefully, gently opening and closing the door, rolling up a floor mat, saying please and thank you, and solving social problems.

An environment like this encourages the development of physical, social, and mental skills and fosters a work ethic that leads to success in later academic work. It has five essential components: physical arrangement, established rituals, peace and serenity, freedom with responsibility, and awareness of and respect for the classroom and other students' personal space.

Physical Arrangement

Classroom shape and design vary in every building; each teacher needs to determine the furniture arrangement that best supports her purpose. Partner teachers

(teachers who each teach in a different language, alternating between the same two groups of students) need to create mirrored classrooms that look and feel the same and have the same purpose and expectations so students moving from one space to the other are comfortable and at ease.

Each primary classroom needs a magic carpet (*alfombra mágica*) on which students can gather for whole-group instruction. A large area rug is ideal, but if one is not available, doormats, cushions, or even placemats can be used. Seating spaces should be assigned to students based on their individual needs. Placing a special chair for the teacher at one edge of the magic carpet creates an inviting ambiance that encourages a love for learning. This group setting may also include a covered table with a decorative lamp, a rocking chair, whimsical furnishings, an easel, a pocket chart, a basket of props, or anything else needed to support instruction. One teacher we know puts on a pair of sparkling ruby slippers during magic carpet time!

An area designed for small-group instruction usually includes a kidney-shaped or round table large enough to accommodate five or six students working in a homogeneous group (at a similar ability level).

Individual and small-group work is facilitated by open shelves (so they don't block anyone's ability to see or be seen) of reachable height, labeled by content area (or center), large enough to store a minimum of six shelf activities per area without crowding or clutter. In kindergarten, these content areas include library, language arts, math, science, social studies, life skills, technology, and art. In first grade, art and life skills are integrated into thematic units, but the other content areas remain. Shelf activities in first grade are designed to develop precooperative social skills either in pairs or groups of four. Cooperative manipulation of materials and oral discussion stimulate critical-thinking skills such as analysis, synthesis, and evaluation. They also strengthen communication skills and promote language acquisition in a natural setting. First-grade shelf activities lay the developmental foundation needed to support cooperative learning in second grade. Shelf activities are replaced by centers in second grade and become more product based. Second-grade students move through centers in groups of four with only one center activity per content area, which is theme based and changes every week. Students at centers work cooperatively, sometimes producing a single product as a team, sometimes each producing an individual product to hand in to the teacher to be graded. In third through fifth grades, product-based centers are replaced by process-based centers (which are explained in Step 4) and provide students with opportunities to think freely through explorations, inventions, and challenges.

In kindergarten and first grade, students have small, lightweight, stackable chairs, which they can manipulate in order to develop gross motor skills, fine motor skills, and good posture for writing activities. The library center is a cozy, comfortable area perfect for casual reading. It may include pillows, mats, beanbag chairs, and an audience of dolls and stuffed animals to read to. There is ample floor space on which to engage in activities, and students can stand up to work on pocket charts, word walls, and bulletin boards. Children, like adults, need to be able to move and change positions.

In second through fifth grades, small tables of four are still preferred to facilitate the group discussions at the heart of cooperative learning; however, when tables are not available, four student desks can be arranged to create a square. If space is limited, center activities may be stored in containers and distributed when needed.

Established Rituals

Classroom routines give students a sense of security and well-being. This security heightens students' self-esteem, because they know what they are expected to do and can accomplish their goals. Time is used efficiently because transitions occur quickly. Teachers model classroom rituals and also provide direct instruction in how they go until students understand the expectations and can take on the responsibility of directing their own instruction. All expectations must be taught: morning greeting, moving within the classroom, lining up, hanging up backpacks and lunch pails, writing in journals, sharing daily news, filing and storing completed work, choosing where to work on activities, solving problems at the peace table, keeping center activity shelves in order, rotating between classrooms, and so on. Teachers cannot expect behavior from students that they have not modeled and taught.

Partner teachers must plan these rituals together so that their classrooms are consistent. Students cannot be expected to learn a different set of procedures with each teacher. Communication and teamwork between partner teachers are essential in establishing expectations and providing students with a predictable daily schedule.

Each room should have a pocket chart that clearly describes each classroom job (in kindergarten each description should be accompanied by an illustration). The teacher can indicate who does what by putting name-labeled clothespins, cards, or Popsicle sticks into the appropriate pockets. These jobs allow students to own their classroom and help teachers modify behavior. Students with behavior problems can be assigned jobs that focus on practical life skills. Job assignments should of course be rotated, and once a child has been trained to do a job, he can be responsible for training his successor. Sophisticated labels for these jobs—language specialist, math engineer, librarian, botanist, zoologist, inspector, supervisor, sanitary engineer, scientist, diplomat—add a sense of importance, build vocabulary, and promote career awareness. Students may apply for jobs and be hired by their teachers. They can be fired, although disciplinary action should be taken first.

Each day ends on the magic carpet as students review what they have learned that day, evaluate their work, and predict what they will learn the next day. Teachers can then dismiss students, group by group, to get backpacks, get their homework folders, pack up their backpacks and lunch pails, stack their chairs, and line up for dismissal. Allow enough time for warm, cheerful good-byes.

Peace and Serenity

The classroom should be peaceful and serene. Teachers' quiet and soothing tone demonstrates the expected noise level in the classroom. It is through their teachers' consistent modeling that students understand the acceptable levels of indoor voices. Although the classroom is quiet, it is not silent. Teachers encourage students to engage in conversations while sharing their thoughts and ideas and communicating orally in two languages. However, all transitions happen in silence so they'll take place more quickly and students can remain focused on academic studies.

Managing their behavior helps students develop needed social skills so teachers can focus on teaching rather than punishing—teachers can empower students by teaching them the skills they need to solve their own problems.

Classroom Meetings

A community of learners develops standards for acceptable behavior through the forum of classroom meetings. Students learn diplomacy, develop the ability to solve their own problems, and are motivated to monitor themselves. They are allowed to act as their own agents. Since each student is an equal participant in a class meeting, sitting in a circle eliminates any sense of hierarchy and encourages individual validation. Students demonstrate respect for one another by speaking one at a time while others listen. Each person may give an opinion and be heard. The class makes decisions by consensus when possible and by majority rule if a consensus cannot be reached.

Through class meetings children develop a vested interest in the classroom community. The meetings cultivate positive feelings toward and encouragement of and by others. Misconduct is discussed and dealt with, and peers provide new options for behavior and support when needed.

The class meeting begins with a sharing of compliments: student to student, student to self, teacher to students, and students to teacher. Initially, compliments will be superficial, and the teacher will need to model meaningful remarks. Eye contact is essential when giving and receiving compliments. All compliments are answered with a thank-you. Character-building vocabulary such as *compassionate*, *courtesy*, and *empathy* can be taught directly. Some days student sharing can take the place of compliments: "Today, my goal is . . ." This is followed by old business and then by future plans. The assignment of classroom jobs is discussed and changed. Concerns or problems that have been placed on a list or in a suggestion box are addressed, and the cohesive group solves them together. Tattling and complaining are eliminated once students understand that the class meeting includes a specific time for solving problems and that the focus is on solutions, not consequences.

Patience and building community are keys to a well-functioning classroom meeting. It is important that students own the rules, enforcing them through problem solving and mediation.

The Thinking Chair and the Peace Table

Every classroom should include a space to which students can go to reflect on their inappropriate actions. The time spent in this *thinking chair* is determined by the age of the child. (Some type of timer may be helpful.) The student in the thinking chair is not allowed to interrupt the teacher or the students. When the time-out ends, the teacher asks the student whether she has come up with a solution for the inappropriate action and is ready to rejoin the group. If the child responds negatively, the teacher might assign additional time or he might impose more severe consequences.

Each classroom also needs an area designated for interpersonal negotiation, called the *peace table*. Students in conflict can sit across from each other, jointly touching a revered object such as a white flower or a special box. They talk about how they feel about each other's actions, negotiate a compromise, and plan a peaceful solution. When introducing the peace table, the teacher models hand-shaking, eye contact, and phrases such as "I do not like it when you . . ." "I am feeling . . ." "I am sorry," and "Thank you."

Freedom with Responsibility

The balance between freedom and responsibility is essential. A teacher's job is to hold a deep respect for each child's unique needs and abilities and meet those needs and make use of those abilities. Content-based activity centers include a number of activities from which students are free to choose based on their developmental needs. Through observation, encouragement, direction, and redirection, teachers acknowledge and respect each student's choice. Teachers also establish, model, and teach step-by-step procedures for completing each activity in a way that meets its objectives. Students are allowed to investigate and explore materials and expand an activity if they can; however, the activities are not toys but a means to acquire knowledge. Students learn to value class work and always

Peace Table

label it appropriately, as *work*. Developing a good work ethic begins at a very young age. The ability and willingness to work are marks of a happy, well-adjusted person. Through accomplishment, children develop an inner sense of peace and contentment.

Intrinsic Motivation

Children are born with an inner drive to learn the skills they need in order to take the next step in their development. A young infant first attempts to lift his head, then rolls over, sits up, pushes up, crawls, stands up, reaches, and finally walks. The motivation for this comes from an inner desire to develop freedom and independence. These developmental needs are also evident in the classroom. One academic skill builds on the next, motivating the student intrinsically to continue learning. Teachers need to cultivate positive feelings and encourage learning. Self-esteem is built when students recognize their accomplishments. Students develop a love of learning.

Extrinsic Motivation

Students may also be rewarded and motivated with tangible objects like stickers, coupons, money, and food. Although extrinsic motivation and behavior modification are sometimes necessary for students who lack self-control, tangible rewards should in general be used only with students who have special needs.

Cooperative Learning

Cooperative learning is most appropriate for students in the second through twelfth grades. It teaches students the interpersonal skills they need in order to function productively in the workforce and participate in a democratic society. Cooperative learning emphasizes the *process* of learning rather than *what* is learned. Students by nature want to question, discuss, argue, and share. Student discourse like this is essential in fostering language acquisition. Cooperative learning encourages interaction among team members. Students rely on one another to get a task accomplished; they learn from and teach one another; they guide one another's explorations; they engage in multisensory activities. They also develop a positive interdependence; all team members participate in and are accountable for what is being and has been learned (Johnson and Johnson 1999).

Awareness of the Classroom

It can be difficult for experienced teachers to relinquish teacher-directed instruction. In dual language immersion, teachers are observers, recorders, planners, and facilitators of learning. Their job is to establish a student-directed classroom that meets the developmental needs of all of its students. The students are empowered by a well-prepared and well-organized environment rich in opportunities to learn. The teachers provide materials and step-by-step directions to enable students to do their assigned jobs. With students taking part in group and independent learning, teachers can focus on monitoring all students, recording their observations and assessments on the run (see Step 6).

> Creating the right environment at school is as important as what I teach. By providing a safe environment, I foster a positive self-image, I allow children to become independent, and I create an environment in which students develop a love for learning. These elements are important in children's development because they give children the tools they need to be confident and successful in life. Because I believe children function best in an organized and structured setting, I go to great lengths to ensure that my classroom meets these criteria. My experiences have shown me that in a setting like this, children learn to work both collaboratively and independently and do so with very little teacher-directed instruction. Regardless of which learning direction they choose, ultimately it leads to self-discovery, self-challenge, mastery of skills, and a greater desire to reach their potential.
>
> —*Amy Turk, dual language teacher and mentor,*
> *J. Marlan Walker International School*

Summary

An aesthetically pleasing classroom elevates children's spirits. A practical class-room facilitates flexible groupings. Working individually, with a partner, and in groups, students develop the social skills needed to accept responsibility for their actions. Training students in the workings of the classroom during the first few weeks of school sets a tone and establishes an environment that guarantee children's developmental needs will be met.

Step 3

Planning Instruction

Children have a real understanding only of that which they invent themselves, and each time we try to teach them too quickly, we keep them from reinventing it themselves.

—Jean Piaget

Journal Entry
February 3, 2005

Today we started the unit on Life Cycles. Two mother helpers had stayed after school to help me on Friday and we transformed our classroom by changing the theme bulletin board and clearing the theme word wall. I brought in the egg incubator, the aquarium for tadpoles, and the lighted plant holder. This took a little rearranging of furniture. I feel so fortunate to have parent support. My partner, these two moms, and I made this transformation of both classrooms in one hour's time. Having the support of collected instructional materials available in our unit bins makes life so doable. I don't have to go gathering from here and there. Our grade-level team organization is a key component to making this work. It has been difficult for some teachers to conform, but through peer pressure they now are held accountable. When it is my turn for a unit I refuse to accept it from the last partner teachers until they have organized well. All parts and pieces must be accounted for, replacement parts must be ordered, and dated order forms included. My partner and I do the same before we pass the unit to the next teachers.

The creative side of me had great fun planning activities and lessons for this unit. Once my partner and I started we took delight in making everything relate and connect. Our classrooms seemed to maintain individuality and yet are so related. The children will experience the germination of duck eggs in my partner's room and chicken eggs in mine. They will watch beans sprout at her table and grow radishes in mine. This ability to observe and compare likes and differences is what research has proven to be one of the most effective strategies of teaching. I feel good about this instruction and yet I feel comfortable in my classroom space with room to move and facilitate independent student learning. I removed everything from the class that did not immediately support this unit of study. My students will be able to focus on the current concepts being developed. I packed up everything from last month's unit and gave it to the next set of partner teachers

from our flow chart. It all had a place to go and be used once again. Just imagine if I had to store all of these things in my room, OH MY! talk about claustrophobic!

—*Second-Grade Teacher*

The third step in dual language immersion is planning collaborative instruction. Our sixteen years of brainstorming and planning as coworkers, sharing thoughts, ideas, and experiences, have produced the paradigm shift described in this book. We have reached the obvious conclusion that two brains are better than one, that partner teaching is powerful, and that the synergy of grade-level team planning can be explosive.

Pat Dragan, author of *A How-to Guide for Teaching English Language Learners: In the Primary Classroom* (2005), notes that she taught in several instructional situations where teachers shared classes and did a great deal of planning together. All of these programs were configured differently and featured team teaching, but none were dual language experiences. In dual language immersion programs, two teachers usually collaborate, plan, and deliver instruction. Students in the programs spend half their day acquiring academic content in English, the other half acquiring academic content in a language other than English. The partner teachers exchange students at midday. However, since in most cases morning and afternoon sessions are not of equal length, students who receive English instruction in the morning one week receive their morning instruction in the non-English language the next week, and vice versa.

At our school, grade-level teams prepare a series of integrated units on informational topics that specifically address the social studies and science standards, which are then rotated and shared among partner teacher teams. A curricular unit may consist of big books, trade books, interactive books, books on tape, multiple copies of leveled books for small-group instruction, center activities, bulletin board visuals, calendars, manipulatives, games, software, stories, poems, experiments, maps, masks and props for plays, flannel boards, puppets, flash cards, sentence strips, and so on, in both languages of instruction. The basic skills of reading, writing, and arithmetic are integrated into the units.

Through these units, students make connections between academic skills and real life. For example, when studying a unit on plants, students may be given a math problem of dividing a handful of seeds equally among six pots of soil. In the same unit, they practice comprehension by reading the directions on the seed package in order to determine how deep and how far apart to plant the seeds. Recording seed germination and plant growth in a daily journal teaches them how to sequence information in writing. Using computers, students draw pictures of the different stages of growth from seed to mature plant, support each illustration with a statement or two, and create a PowerPoint presentation, which becomes an alternative assessment demonstrating students' mastery of sequencing, writing, and technology. A curricular unit word wall enriches students' academic vocabulary as well as their spelling, reading, and writing skills.

This interconnection of academic subjects allows partner teachers to move their students comfortably from the English classroom to the non-English classroom and back again. The two classrooms support each other with a constant flow of instruction and learning devoted to the same theme.

Thematic instruction requires that the climate and mood of the classroom support the topic being studied. When students enter the classroom on the first day of a new unit, it is evident that they are about to start out on an exciting new venture. Visuals capture the students' interest and draw their focus: books related to the theme are displayed on the easel and in the classroom library; the bulletin board sports labeled illustrations and key facts. Activity centers offer opportunities to explore the topic. Manipulatives are often geared to the topic. (For example, for a unit on insects, the manipulatives in the math center might be plastic bugs, and number cards might display dragonflies or ladybugs.) Sometimes teachers wear historical costumes. Introducing a fifth-grade unit on explorers, one teacher arrived dressed as Ponce de Leon. However, it is wise to remember that simplicity is key. A cluttered classroom can over-stimulate the students and prevent them from focusing on the learning objectives.

Partner Teacher Planning

A working partnership is a powerful tool for less experienced teachers, because being able to share responsibilities lowers the stress they experience. As much as possible, each teacher teaches alone in her own classroom, but the two plan instruction, determine grades, and prepare their rooms as a team. Thorough planning is essential. Partners can brainstorm, bounce ideas around, and predetermine possible weaknesses before they teach the lessons. It is also essential that partner teachers be able to plan their instruction together, at the same time—either before or after school or during a mutual free period.

Currently, the No Child Left Behind legislation mandates that every child's individual needs be addressed and planned for. Individual assessments, as described in Step 6, provide the data needed to plan for each student. Based on this information, teachers predetermine instruction required by homogenous small groups as well as the depth and breadth of center activities.

In creating their integrated instruction, partner teachers use a two-page web organizer. The center circle on each page defines the theme. Surrounding rectangles identify core curriculum areas: reading, writing, math, social studies, science, and technology. In each subject rectangle on the first page, the teachers write the standards to be mastered during the unit. On the second page, the teachers use the boxes to brainstorm instructional activities, divided equally between them, that are correlated to the identified standards. (Appendix C contains a sample web graphic organizer for a primary-grade unit on insects.)

In a one-way dual language program, the minority language teacher (teaching in the students' second language) presents the activities that are more concrete and more easily demonstrated or dramatized. The majority language teacher (teaching in the students' dominant language) presents the activities that are more abstract and require conceptual explanations.

In order for students to comprehend new concepts, the minority language teacher must provide plenty of support through manipulatives, pictures, real objects, and graphic organizers, showing as well as telling. This type of instruction is best for all students, but it is essential for students learning in a second language. Here's an example. When teaching students how to determine the total monetary value of a group of coins and bills, the majority language teacher would start by finding out what students already know about what various coins and bills are worth and model adding up those values. The minority language teacher would give students facsimiles of the coins and bills to examine and touch as he, using the second language, modeled identifying the values and adding them up. Students would learn the appropriate vocabulary in a natural setting while at the same time mastering the academic objective of determining the total value.

In two-way immersion, activities can be equally divided based on teacher preferences. The partner teachers plan activities that parallel and support each other. They do not repeat the same activity in both classrooms.

Curricular Units in a Nutshell

The topics of units must be broad, be significant, accommodate a variety of instructional strategies, and prompt students to inquire, reflect, think, and feel. Schoolwide planning, both at and across grade levels, is important: students should not encounter the same topics in different grades. Kindergarten units are scheduled for two-week rotations. Here are some suggestions for thematic unit topics:

Kindergarten
The Alphabet
Nursery Rhymes
Seasons
Me
Pumpkins
The Farm
Gingerbread
Dinosaurs
Five Senses
Animals
The Human Body
Bears
The World
Mexico
Trees
Fabrics
Wood and Paper

First Grade
Classic Stories/Fairy Tales
Food/Nutrition
My Family and Me
Community and Maps
Safety
Plants
Balance and Motion
The Spanish-Speaking World
Pebbles, Sand, and Silt: Ocean and
    Desert

Second Grade
Space
Life Cycles
Birds
Sound
Rocks
Insects
Air and Weather
Solids and Liquids
Transportation
Immigration Patterns

Third Grade
Habitats
Ecosystems
Light and Heat
Physics and Sound
Structure of Life
Measurement
Earth Materials/Rocks
Environmental Effects on
    Indigenous People

Fourth Grade
Myths and Fables
Westward Movement

Fifth Grade
The Food Chain
Civil War

Inventions	World Civilizations
Water	Explorers
Magnets and Electricity	Castles/Feudal System
Landforms	Speeches
Systems of the Human Body	The Renaissance
Economic Systems	Government Systems
Alternative Energy Sources	Mixtures/Solutions

Units can be reused year after year if the materials are carefully packed and stored in labeled, sealed containers. (Big books that do not fit into the bins can be stored separately and labeled by topic.) An inventory should be posted inside the lid, with items that need to be replaced highlighted. The responsibility of caring for the materials falls on all teachers as a cooperative team who depend on one another to value, respect, and preserve mutual property. A rotation system should be developed by which each team of partner teachers is allotted an appropriate amount of time to use every thematic unit appropriate to their grade level. Filing each team's two-page graphic organizer in a notebook that accompanies each unit lets teachers build on the plans of others, enhancing the unit with everyone's ideas and inspirations.

> In planning and preparing a thematic unit, partner teachers need to devote a significant amount of time to learning centers and the overall classroom atmosphere. Rooms should "mirror" each other in every possible aspect in order to stimulate language growth and connection.
>
> —*Second-grade partner teachers at J. Marlan Walker International School*

> Constant communication is essential for successful partner teaching. Sharing every day allows partner teachers to identify the learning styles of all their students and thus provide them with appropriate instruction.
>
> —*Barbara Friday and Anita Pisano, second-grade partner teachers, J. Marlan Walker International School*

Unit Bins

Summary

Teaching using curricular units is just plain fun! Students learn at an accelerated pace, as the basic skills of reading, writing, and arithmetic are incorporated into content-area units. Children can watch eggs hatch into baby chicks; observe the development of tadpoles into frogs; read about the adventures of Marco Polo; investigate the effects of electricity on civilization; or compare and contrast communism, capitalism, monarchies, and dictatorships. In one kindergarten classroom we visited recently, the children explained the purpose of a pancreas, challenging us to rethink the limited expectations we sometimes have for the children we teach.

Teaching Through Best Practice

*To be a teacher you must be a prophet because you are trying
to prepare people for a world thirty to fifty years into the
future.*

—Gordon Brown

Journal Entry
September 10, 2005

This Saturday morning the coffee was brewing, the breakfast and snacks spread of
bagels and fruits made a lovely table. Someone brought in fresh flowers and a
cheery tablecloth. It feels like home! I guess the school is my second home. There
we were my school colleagues and I bonding with each other laughing, teasing,
and creating memorable times. It was our turn for learning. The staff developers
put cooperative learning structures in place to model "good teaching" in action.
As teachers we were experiencing the students' roles. I realized that as a learner I
need a low stress environment, frequent movement opportunities, and noticed
the diversity of learning styles in my group. I guess I can never just assume learning will happen, I need to learn how to make it happen!

—*First-Grade Teacher*

Teacher preparation programs of the past focused on preparing professionals to disseminate content knowledge to their students. But in a world where what there is to know is growing exponentially every day, teachers need to learn how to give their students opportunities to acquire information; show them how to analyze, synthesize, and evaluate that information; and moderate discussions, debates, and presentations in which students share information and learn from one another.

In dual language immersion programs, teacher collaboration is essential. As noted earlier, students in the programs spend half of their day acquiring academic content in English, the other half acquiring academic content in a language other than English, and they switch teachers at midday.

Morning Instruction (Kindergarten and First and Second Grades)

Greeting

The morning schedule (see Figure 4–1) begins with the morning greeting. The teacher stands at the doorway with a welcoming smile. She makes eye contact with each child while shaking hands and speaking in a soft voice. This gesture is a reminder that courteous behavior is expected in school. It is a display of mutual respect and allows students to practice social skills required out in the world. Students then prepare for the day by depositing their homework folders, lunch pails (or lunch money), and backpacks in the appropriate spots. They collect their journals, choose a table at which to sit, and begin the day. These morning routines are accomplished quietly, but students are encouraged to greet one another. Routines and procedures like these help students become self-directed and allow the

---

1. teacher-student greetings with handshakes and eye contact
2. journal writing (thinking, drawing, telling, writing, reading)
        OR (alternate days)
   the writing process (prewriting, drafting, revising, editing, publishing)
3. whole-group instruction (daily news, shared reading, modeled writing, direct math instruction, center activity demonstrations, science experiments)
4. small-group instruction (guided reading, center activities)
5. whole-group instruction (integrated thematic lesson)
6. wrap-up (review and song)

Figure 4–1. Morning Schedule (K–2)

teacher a free moment to record attendance and take care of other administrative details.

Journal Writing

The morning continues with journal writing. Students open their journal to the page of the day, write the date, and read the posted prompt or select their own topic. Then they close their eyes and think of what they will share related to the topic.

At the beginning of the year, the teacher models journal writing (a five-step metacognitive process) until the students are able to proceed on their own. The first step is to think about what they are going to write. The second step is to draw a picture of the story they will be writing about. The third step is to tell their story to a partner. The fourth step is to write their story. The fifth and final step is to read their story to a partner. Each step is timed, and the teacher uses a predetermined signal when it's time to move to the next step.

Keeping these personal journals develops creativity, oral communication, writing and reading skills and meets content-area objectives such as sequencing, letter formation, and punctuation. The journals themselves are a cumulative record of student writing. When teachers write in their own journals as the students write in theirs, they provide a valuable model.

Students often have difficulty thinking of a topic, and their writing can become redundant and unexpressive. One possible solution is to have students bring in movie ticket stubs, Chinese cookie fortunes, party favors, airplane tickets, shopping receipts, clothes tags, and the like and keep them in personal treasure bags. Sorting through these items can remind students of memorable times they can write about.

The Writing Process

Teachers often alternate journal writing with writing that implements the five recursive steps of the writing process. During *prewriting*, students generate ideas, conceptualize thoughts, and activate their prior knowledge. In *drafting*, students determine their purpose and put their ideas on paper. While *revising*, students research, problem solve, and organize. They clarify and refine their papers during the *editing* phase. Typically, students cycle through these steps multiple times as they work to create a meaningful written piece; the steps don't mean to imply a neat, linear progression. Finally, in *publishing* their piece, students present it to a selected audience.

Whole-Group Instruction

Students put away their journal and silently move to their designated spot on the magic carpet. The teacher sits in the special chair located at the edge of the carpet.

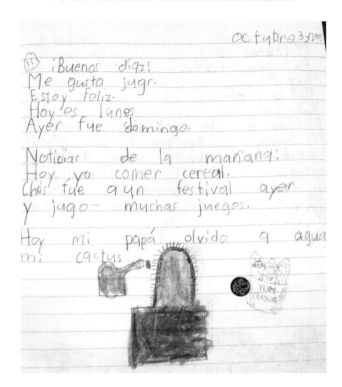

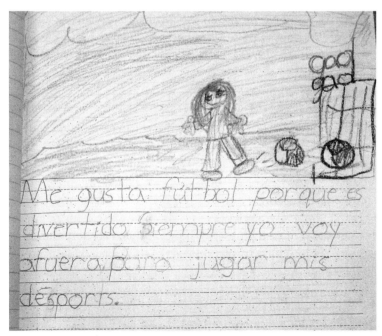

Five-Step Journal Entries

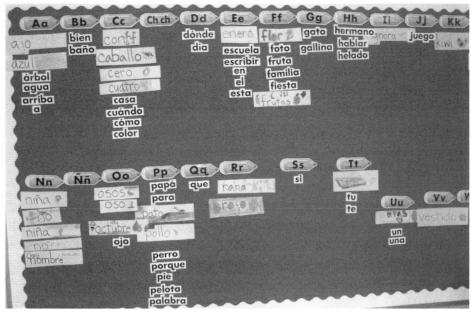

Illustrated Word Wall

The session begins with some daily news: on a chart a student or the teacher writes several sentences describing a personal current event. Then class members read the sentences, discuss them if they wish, and correct any errors they notice. Afterward, there are a few minutes of math practice using the wall calendar. Additional whole-group instruction might include shared reading, modeled writing, math instruction, a center activity demonstration, or a science experiment.

A shared reading lesson is similar to a comfortable, nurturing bedtime story. The teacher models reading strategies and discusses the meaning of the text. Students make predictions about what will happen and confirm or revise those predictions as the story unfolds. According to Routman (1991), shared reading is any rewarding reading situation in which a learner or group of learners sees the text, observes an expert reading it with fluency and expression, and is invited to read along. Shared reading begins with a picture walk that suggests the meaning of the story and encourages predictions; then the teacher reads print. The cloze technique is often used during the reading: the teacher pauses before a predictable word and encourages children to read the word utilizing the illustrations and their sense of story. Through shared reading, children develop concepts of print and become familiar with the parts of a book. Students learn about left-to-right directionality, the sequence of events, words and spaces, capitalized and lowercase letters, reading from top to bottom, and using illustrations to support the print. They

Magic Carpet

learn letter-sound relationships and how to use vocal intonation and dramatic expression. Teaching is accomplished through demonstrations and discussions. The teacher might ask individual students to interact with the text using their fingers, Wikki Stix, removable labels, and pointers. Whole-group interaction may include chants, raps, pantomime, and drama. Big books, songs, poems, graphs, time lines—anything in print—can be used as the springboard for shared reading.

In modeled writing, the teacher shows children how to write by forming print correctly, using appropriate spacing between words, and using correct punctuation. The teacher thinks aloud, models the conventions of print, and uses letter-sound relationships as he forms words. He may deliberately exaggerate the sounds of the blended letters as he forms the written words.

Small-Group Instruction

Next, the students move on to small-group or individual work. In small-group instruction, the teacher pulls together homogeneous groups of students and addresses their specific needs. Working on their own, students complete activities that support their whole-group instruction and record their thinking, take notes, and summarize in content-based journals.

In guided reading, the teacher works with a small homogeneous group of students using a book at their skill level. Based on daily observations and interactions, the teacher chooses a text that offers each child a manageable number of challenges. The aim is to develop independent readers who question, consider alternatives, and make informed choices as they pursue meaning. Guided reading is based on the understanding that readers bring meaning to and gain meaning from the text. Reading the author's message becomes a way for readers to explore and discover themselves and their world. The teacher uses questions and comments to help children become aware of resources within themselves and in the text and use them to overcome difficulties.

The students' guided reading books are sent home in personalized RAH RAH (reading at home) folders. These protective folders include a reading log, a list of ways one might respond to literature, and suggestions for how parents can help their children read at home (Galassi 2002).

Thematic Lesson and Wrap-Up

Finally, the class returns to the magic carpet for an integrated lesson in science, social studies, or math. These lessons are best when they are hands-on. Academic vocabulary is emphasized and is supported by a word wall. (Appendix C is a sample thematic unit with lesson activities designed specifically for a dual language classroom.)

The morning ends with a short review of the information that has been taught, and then everyone sings a favorite song.

Afternoon Instruction (Kindergarten and First and Second Grades)

In the afternoon (see Figure 4–2), students receive instruction in the other language in another classroom with another teacher. Instructional groupings and time frames (except for journal writing) are identical to the morning. The partner teachers have the same instructional objectives but use different instructional approaches and activities.

The afternoon begins with fifteen minutes of student-chosen silent sustained reading. Students then move to the magic carpet for whole-group instruction, which involves either a read-aloud or a shared-writing lesson.

---

1. silent sustained reading (with student-chosen texts)
2. whole-group instruction (read-aloud, shared writing)
3. small-group instruction (guided reading, center activities)
4. whole-group instruction (integrated thematic lesson)
5. wrap-up (short review and song)

Figure 4–2. Afternoon Schedule (K–2)

By reading aloud material the students could not read on their own, the teacher models fluency and exposes them to various genres. After introducing the text by talking about its structure and any necessary background information, the teacher reads it aloud, start to finish. During subsequent readings, she stops to ask and answer questions as necessary. Finally, the teacher asks students which words they don't understand and provides pictures, translations, or definitions. Reading aloud is a good way to familiarize students with a text before having them read it on their own. It also models correct pronunciation, phrasing, and expression (McCloskey 1999). While reading aloud, teachers might also focus on cultural enrichment, developing students' knowledge and interest in things like nursery rhymes, Aesop's fables, language study, history, and natural science.

In shared writing, the teacher and the students jointly compose a paragraph, song, poem, or other text. One way to approach shared writing is through *language experience*. Students first engage in some kind of activity: take a field trip, observe an object or a piece of art, or make cookies, for example. Then they take turns stating the sequence of events orally as the teacher records their statements. For example:

John said, "We measured the flour."
Maria said, "We poured the flour into the bowl."
Sara said, "We poured the milk into the bowl."

Then the teacher and students edit the text together, as the teacher steers them toward the correct language structures and print conventions (McCloskey 1999). Photocopies of the text can be used for follow-up activities that pinpoint phonics, language structure, comprehension, independent reading, and creative expression. Shared writing gives students a sense of ownership and the security that comes with being able to read their own verbal responses.

The afternoon instruction ends with guided reading, center activities, integrated thematic instruction, and a wrap-up, as in the morning.

Second Grade

After two years of precooperative classroom instruction (in kindergarten and first grade), second graders spend a year becoming familiar with and trying out the cooperative learning structures used in third through fifth grades. They begin this transitional year by producing a product at centers to be handed in for a grade. Their teachers explicitly teach social skills such as *respect*, *responsibility*, *discipline*, and *patience*, which are a necessary part of cooperative learning. These skills ensure more effective social interaction. When this foundation is solid, the teacher gradually introduces cooperative learning structures and activities.

Morning Instruction (Third, Fourth, and Fifth Grades)

In intermediate dual language immersion programs, students sometimes have the same bilingual teacher throughout the day. This teacher alternates languages between the morning and the afternoon, staying true to the language of instruction during each time period. Another option is to teach some subjects in one language and some in the other, always integrating reading and writing skills and language development.

Given the increased maturity and sophistication of this age group, teacher-facilitated, student-directed instruction is enhanced. Tables or desks are arranged to accommodate groups of four for cooperative learning. Entering the classroom (in silence, except for polite, friendly greetings), students unpack their backpacks, store them, take out their journals, and begin to work (see Figure 4–3).

Dialogue Journals

Dialogue journals are written to an audience who reads and replies to the entries. This audience may include the teacher, a fellow group member, or another classmate. Writers share life experiences, opinions, feelings, and thoughts. Teachers provide a variety of prompts or let students chose their own topics; in either case the topics should be stimulating and important. The teacher reviews the journals, assessing voice and creativity rather than grammar and syntax.

Lore used a dialogue journal to make a connection with a student from a small town in Mexico who had recently immigrated to the United States. He wrote about his yearning for the rural community he had left. He missed his horses and swimming in the river and mostly the freedom he had lost by moving to a city his parents considered dangerous. Lore shared similar memories of her summer visits to grandparents in Mexico, when she played freely in the countryside with her cousins. She also shared her struggles as a young child unable to speak English in an all-English classroom and encouraged this student to take advantage of the opportunities he would experience in this country. She let him know that she was available to provide whatever support he needed.

---

1. interactive, or dialogue, journals
2. reading workshop
3. process-based centers
4. cultural enrichment lessons
5. short review

Figure 4–3. Morning Schedule (Grades 3–5)

Reading Workshop

Next, students develop their literacy in a reading workshop. The teacher first presents a whole-group minilesson on a specific aspect of reading. Students then read (independently, with a partner, or in small groups) a text they have selected (with the teacher's guidance) that matches their level of fluency. (Researcher Donald Graves [1991] recommends that students be allowed to select for themselves about 80 percent of the texts they read.) During this time the teacher works with individuals or small groups, showing them how to construct meaning, noting their fluency, and assessing their comprehension. These observations are fundamental to individualized language arts instruction. Students who are not reading at grade level will require guided reading instruction. As in earlier grades, students' reading materials are sent home in personalized RAH RAH (reading at home) folders (Galassi 2002) as homework.

Process-Based Centers

As students finish their reading workshop assignments, they choose a process-based center (there are usually six or seven) in which to work. The teacher introduces these centers during Monday morning's whole-group instruction, and they must be completed by the end of the week. Their purpose is to give students the opportunity to explore, let them make their own discoveries, and stimulate their curiosity. The emphasis is not on learning facts but on developing higher-level thinking skills. (Center activities are addressed in Step 5.)

Cultural Enrichment

The morning concludes with a cultural enrichment lesson in a subject such as language arts, fine arts, history, or science. In a whole-group *seminar*, the students and their teacher examine ideas and values related to the topic. In this interactive environment, students acquire knowledge and come to see themselves as critical thinkers by way of dialogue. The teacher guides the proceedings through open-ended questions. For a seminar to be effective, students need to study the topic carefully, listen closely to the comments of others, think critically for themselves, and articulate both their own thoughts and their responses to the thoughts of others. From the students' point of view, the seminar differs from most other formal classroom experiences in that it asks them to voice and examine their own thinking, not replay the thoughts of their teacher or a textbook (Roberts and Staff of the National Paideia Center 1998).

In a fourth-grade cultural enrichment lesson on economics, students role-played living under communism in the former USSR. The teacher, acting as the government, which has total control of money and property, assigned students jobs or careers that included doctors, secretaries, clerks, janitors, farm workers, and teachers. Students received play-money salaries from the government bank based on the number of people in their family and their needs rather than the amount of skill or education their job required or the amount of work they performed. Students set up family budgets and paid their bills. Afterward, students discussed the pros and cons. The next day they simulated life under capitalism. On the third day, they summarized their feelings and experiences about both communism and capitalism using a Venn diagram.

Afternoon Instruction (Third, Fourth, and Fifth Grades)

The afternoon session (see Figure 4–4) begins with the teacher reading aloud for twenty minutes. Next, in a teacher-directed whole-group math lesson, new concepts are introduced using manipulatives. Cooperative learning takes place at intervals as the teacher pauses to allow students to think about their learning, turn to a classmate, and quickly discuss what they have learned.

The teacher then presents science and social studies lessons on alternate days. Again, cooperative learning techniques promote student interaction. Content-based vocabulary is emphasized and displayed on the word wall. Presentations are assessed. Science lessons are hands-on and experiment based. Social studies seminars are investigative and thought provoking. Technology is part of both areas. Students hone their computer skills while researching on the Internet, preparing presentations with PowerPoint, filming experiments and skits, sending and receiving emails, and generating reports.

The afternoon ends with a writing workshop. Students have the opportunity to respond to their reading by highlighting or underlining important imformation, taking notes, making entries in reading notebooks, and writing letters. The teacher begins each writing workshop with a minilesson on a specific aspect of writing. Then, as students work on their projects, the teacher monitors their work,

1. read–aloud
2. direct instruction in math
3. science or social studies theme-based lesson
4. writing workshop
5. brief review

Figure 4–4. Afternoon Schedule (Grades 3–5)

records their progress, and guides them through the writing process from prewriting through publishing. When students finish a piece, they present it to their classmates from the author's chair. Finally, a brief review wraps up the day.

Instructional Strategies for Language Acquisition

Language acquisition strategies must be part of all teacher-directed whole-group and small-group instruction. In a two-way dual language immersion program, half of the students are acquiring knowledge through their second language at any given time. The methods and strategies used for instruction are consistent in both classrooms.

Because instruction in dual language immersion classrooms hinges on language development, teachers need to use strategies that support language acquisition. Every lesson has both a content-based and a language-based objective. Success in these classrooms depends on students' ability to comprehend instruction. Students understand lessons when the teacher shows as well as tells and provides additional low-risk support as necessary.

For example, in a second-grade thematic unit on seasons, the teacher began by building background knowledge through the shared reading of books that discussed the seasons. The classroom word wall displayed vocabulary related to the seasons (with accompanying illustrations), which students could incorporate into their writing. The teacher extended the students' learning by asking them to create a visual representation of their favorite season and then use this illustration to talk about the season with a partner or their cooperative group. The next step was to compare and contrast their favorite season with their least favorite season by entering short phrases or single words on a Venn diagram.

The teacher can also use gestures and body movement to communicate information, a language acquisition strategy known as total physical response (TPR). When body movement is accompanied by sounds coming from someone's mouth, the learner is able to decipher the meaning of those sounds using many levels of awareness, including phonology, morphology, syntax, and semantics. Students also internalize the pattern of the language in which the sounds are being uttered (Asher 1986).

In TPR, students learn through concrete experiences rather than abstract oral descriptions. Support for meaning can come from a detailed picture or a simple sketch. Information can be presented through charts, graphs, and time lines. Graphic organizers arrange information and give students a way to order their thoughts. Various media and technologies also provide visual support.

Teachers in dual language immersion classrooms adjust their rate and complexity of speech to accommodate the needs of the second language learners. They provide background knowledge before introducing new concepts. They teach and reteach information using different approaches to meet individual students' preferred way of thinking, processing, and understanding information. (Learners score *significantly higher* on tests when the material has been presented in a way that honors their preferred style of learning.) A report by the New York State Board of Regents' Panel on Learning Styles states that it is essential to alter teaching strategies to meet the needs of a more multicultural global society (Jensen 1995).

In dual language immersion, academic vocabulary is isolated and explicitly taught to ensure knowledge of key concepts. Teachers choose the most important words from reading selections to add to word walls and use in word-study activities. These words are essential to understanding the text and useful enough that students will read them again in other books.

Students in dual language immersion programs take an active role in their learning. They acquire language naturally, by being physically and mentally involved in meaningful, relevant activities. Krashen and Terrell (1983) have identified these key principles in the natural approach to learning:

- Instruction focuses on communication rather than form.
- Speech production comes slowly and is never forced.
- Early speech has natural stages (yes-or-no responses, one-word answers, lists of words, short phrases, complete sentences).
- The teacher creates situations in which students are motivated to communicate.
- Instruction must be interesting and comprehensible.
- Understanding is more important than speaking.
- Vocabulary development is more important than structural accuracy.
- Errors are not corrected in isolation.
- The learning situation is relaxed, with no anxiety.

Language acquisition occurs in a sequence of three natural stages: comprehension, early speech, and speech emergence. Each stage has its own limits and possibilities, which must be respected and embraced (Freeman Dhority and Jensen 1998).

Best practice includes powerful strategies to help students acquire information and language skills. In a thematic unit on the wetlands in a dual language third-grade classroom, small cooperative learning groups of four students each were assigned to study three types of wetlands—swamps, marshes, and bogs—and the animals and plants living in each. One student's Internet research led her to study the geological processes by which bogs are formed. Another student focused on the specific details that distinguish plant life at the bottom of bogs. One group was fascinated with the fact that nearly five acres of Everglades swamp are disappearing each day. As their teacher, I was challenged to tailor our class discussions to accommodate these far-flung interests. At the unit's end, however, when students shared their research, it was like watching a flock of birds coalesce into perfect formation.

—*Catherine Maack, third-grade dual language teacher,*
J. Marlan Walker International School

Summary

In a dual language immersion program, language acquisition strategies are in constant use. Our challenge as educators, parents, policy makers, and researchers is to ensure that each instructional component and strategy we implement is geared to helping students become completely bilingual and biliterate. How exciting a classroom becomes when the teacher gets to learn and grow alongside his students! Watching their teacher learn, students see how to seek out knowledge and become lifelong learners themselves.

Learning Through Hands-on Activities

I hear and I forget. I see and I remember. I do and I understand.

—Chinese Proverb

Journal Entry
January 16, 2005

I consider the best teaching strategy of this dual language model to be the use of shelf activities. It is because of these shelf activities that I know my students' needs are met. It is my way of challenging, providing remediation, and differentiating instruction. Today I observed Stephen naturally gravitated to the language activity center in order to practice his alphabetizing skills. I saw him repeatedly practicing in order to learn to mastery. I witnessed his inner desire to master this concept.

When my students are working at shelf activities everyone becomes an independent or cooperative learner and no one wastes time. They are completely engaged in the activities and through my observations I can see that they are constantly thinking and are being challenged by these multileveled shelf activities.

—Kindergarten Teacher

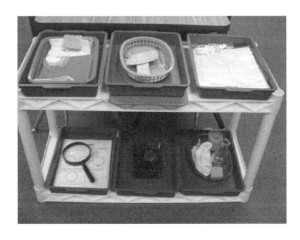

At the core of dual language immersion programs are meaningful hands-on shelf activities that allow students to become actively engaged in learning. They include interactive materials that make abstract concepts clear and concrete. By experimenting with concrete materials, students internalize academic concepts. The world can be grasped only by action, not by contemplation. The hand is more important than the ear and the eye. The hand drives the subsequent evolution of the brain. The hand is the cutting edge of the mind (Bronowski 1974).

In the primary grades, using real tools to perform real jobs encourages children to view themselves as workers rather than pretenders. People who are passionate about their work and who enjoy it are engaged and challenged by their job. When adults find no pleasure in their work, it is usually because it lacks challenge, interest, choice, and variety. Children are no different. Classroom shelf activities provide students with this challenge, interest, choice, and variety.

In the intermediate grades students work at process-based centers inventing, researching, constructing, analyzing, and solving real problems. Workbooks and worksheets don't bring skills and concepts to life. In order for students to gain a true understanding of academic concepts, they must become active learners rather than wait passively for a teacher to provide them with knowledge.

Teachers who observe children notice that they like to mimic adult behavior by doing things for themselves. Children who are allowed to be independent become self-disciplined. Students who are allowed to choose and work on meaningful shelf activities or process-based centers in the classroom develop a sense of worth and forge a work ethic, values that will benefit them throughout their lives. The effective teacher designs shelf activities or process-based centers that support a student-directed classroom, taking into consideration diverse learning styles and providing opportunities for each student to work at her own level. While working on activities, students can move about freely, choose the type of work they will do, and determine whether they will work independently or with others. They are held accountable for demonstrating respect for others, taking care of materials, working in a contained space, and returning activities to the shelves in the condition in which they found them.

The teacher's job is to model and encourage children to become observers of detail. This allows the children to discover knowledge and manage their environment. Rather than teaching facts, the teacher provides the freedom for children to develop interest and enthusiasm in their own work. Children enjoy making choices, exploring, and investigating. However, freedom includes limitations as well as boundaries and is earned through a child's ability to demonstrate responsibility. The teacher needs to make clear the structure and expectations for successful student-directed activities.

According to Maria Montessori, the most striking teaching tool, almost a magic wand, for releasing the normal expression of a child's natural gifts is a task that requires movement of the hands guided by the intellect. Activities like these reveal the true child. We see children kindled with joy and indefatigable in their toil since their activities are intimately connected to their life and growth. Choice is now their guiding principle (Futrell 1998).

Classroom activities are arranged on open, reachable shelves, referred to as *centers*, so that students can access them easily. (If your classroom does not include durable wooden shelving, you can purchase inexpensive plastic shelves at hardware stores.) Each center houses activities related to a specific area of the curriculum: life skills, language arts, math, science, international studies, library, technology, and so on. All of the necessary materials for each activity are stored on a tray or in a box or plastic container. Visual appeal is important: activities must be presented in an orderly, inviting manner.

Content-Based Centers

A content-based (math, language arts, science, etc.) center should have a minimum of six shelf activities, available for at least six weeks (usually coinciding with a thematic unit), designed to give students hands-on practice toward mastering grade-level standards in the subject area. While homogenous (at the same reading level) guided reading groups are receiving small-group instruction, heterogeneous groups of students (ideally, one excellent reader, two average readers, and one struggling reader) rotate through the learning centers at twenty-minute intervals. Students should be allowed to interact and share ideas with one another using whisper voices.

A possible alternative to team rotations is to give individual students weekly menus of activities they need to complete that week. A menu like this allows the teacher to guide children who lack self-direction. It can be created by the teacher, arrived at collaboratively during a student-teacher conference, or written by the student and approved by the teacher. These menus can also be generic, listing all activities in all centers, for students to check off as they complete each one. The approach a teacher takes depends on the level of responsibility students are capable of as well as their ability to be self-directed learners.

Whenever possible, shelf activities should be designed so that students can check and verify their work themselves; activities must also be multileveled in order to meet the needs of diverse learners. Since the practice aspect of an activity is of prime importance, students in a primary classroom can revisit an activity as often as they remain interested in doing so. When children revisit an activity, they may approach it in a different manner and gain a diverse perspective. The teacher may also decide, based on assessment-on-the-run observations (see Step 6), to reteach or enrich the activity or help individual students reflect on their performance and accomplishments.

Teachers model and introduce each activity in a short minilesson before they place it in a center. First they define appropriate work spaces (not in front of doorways or in places that impede the flow of movement in the classroom) and show students how to walk to their work space with their activity container and establish a boundary (usually with a rug or placemat). Then they state and clarify the objectives of the activity, dramatically demonstrating the procedures to be followed, step-by-step. During the minilesson, teachers refer to the activity by name and make sure students know they are expected to call the activity by this name. If the activity can be corrected by students themselves, teachers explain and demonstrate this. At the conclusion of the minilesson, teachers demonstrate how to put the activity back in its storage container and return it to the shelf. Modeling and insisting on careful carrying of materials builds fine and gross motor skills in students and teaches them to move in space gracefully without spills, damages, bumps, falls, or accidents. Children become aware of what they are able to manage as well as respect the boundaries of other people. Allowing children to clean up their own accidents will build self-confidence, poise, and grace.

Sample Math Activity

For a primary-grade integrated unit on trees, a teacher created a math activity using ten blank cards in the shape of trees, ten cards on which either the Spanish number words *uno, dos, tres, cuatro, cinco, seis, siete, ocho, nueve, diez* or the English number words *one, two, three, four, five, six, seven, eight, nine, ten* were written or printed, and fifty-five Velcro apples. Students demonstrate that they under-

Primary Math Shelf Activity

stand the concept that each word signifies a particular quantity by matching the word cards with tree cards to which they have attached the correct number of Velcro apples. (You could also attach Velcro to word cards so that both the words and the apples could be attached to the tree cards.) This activity is self-correcting, because if it is completed properly, there will be no apples left. An enrichment might include removing the cards with the written number words and having the students write the correct number word on a blank card. Another idea is to have students alphabetize the number word cards. If remediation is necessary, teachers could provide a student with a number line from one to ten as a reference for sequencing the cards.

Sample Science Activity

In a science shelf activity, also related to the tree unit, students use a magnifying glass to examine different types of pinecones, the bark of a tree, and a cross-section of a tree trunk. Using their senses as they manipulate and explore the world around them, students notice the difference between the outside (bark) and the inside of the wood. They explore holding the magnifying glass closer to and farther away from the objects and determine the optimal distance. They then record their observations in the content-based journal provided as part of the activity.

Primary Science Shelf Activity

An enrichment activity would be to have students create a list of words describing the organic material they are examining. Or the teacher could provide prompts: *The wood looks like _____. The pinecone smells like _____. The bark feels like _____.* As a remediation, teachers might provide materials for students to do texture rubbings of the items or include word cards to use in the sentence blanks.

Activities from the Early Learning Materials (ELM) Group

Good Vibrations

Materials
- 1 green oval basket
- 1 towel
- 1 sponge
- 1 tuning fork
- 1 50 ml beaker (to be filled with water at the start of the activity)

Question
What will happen to the water when I strike the tuning fork and insert it in the water?

Procedure
Open the towel and place the beaker full of water, the tuning fork, and the sponge on it. Holding the tuning fork by the ball, strike it on the edge of the table and hold it close to your ears. Strike it again and feel it gently with your thumb and index finger. Strike it one more time and hold it gently against the outside rim of the beaker. Strike it a fourth time and place it in water, dipping only the tips. Watch what happens to the water. Dry the tuning fork with the sponge and replace the materials in the basket.

Explanation
When the prongs of the tuning fork are struck, they vibrate. This causes molecules of air around them to vibrate, causing the water to move.

Sink and Float

Materials
- 1 red basket tray
- 1 measuring cup
- 1 petri dish

1 set of six-inch tongs
1 towel
1 sponge
2 cards, one labeled *sink*, the other labeled *float*

Objects
1 medium five-sixteenths-inch bolt
1 cork
1 wooden rod
1 key
1 shell
1 large three-eighths-inch nut
1 clothespin
1 paper clip

Question
What will happen to each of these objects when it is placed in water?

Procedure
Open the towel and center one card over the first half, the other over the second half. Place all of the objects in the petri dish. Fill the measuring cup with one cup of water. Begin dropping the objects in the water one by one. Retrieve the objects from the water using the tongs and place them on the towel under the appropriate card. Review with your teacher which objects float and which objects sink. Dry all materials and equipment and return them to the tray.

Explanation
When an object weighs less than an equal volume of water, it floats; when it weighs more than an equal volume of water, it sinks. The force is called *displacement*.

Phonetic Object Box

Materials
1 four-by-six-inch acrylic box to store miniature objects
1 felt underlayer
1 set of miniature objects
blank labels (laminated ones last longer)

Purpose
To introduce students to the idea that an object has a name that can be written to signify the object

Lesson

1. The teacher spreads out underlayer and places box above it.
2. Take out miniature objects one by one, and review each name.
3. Place the objects on the left side of the underlayer.
4. As the children watch, slowly write the name of one of the objects on a label.
5. After the children have read the word, place it next to the object.
6. Repeat for all of the objects.
7. Have the children read all the labels again.
8. Gather up the labels and have the children read them and then place them next to the correct object.
9. Staple the labels and make them into a booklet the children can use when they practice the activity independently.

Process-Based Centers for Intermediate Grades

The purpose of process-based centers is to stimulate higher-level thinking. Students are required to research, investigate, or explore a concept related to a grade-level curriculum standard and justify, defend, and debate what they discover.

For example, students in an intermediate classroom studying an integrated thematic unit on inventions might be given a toy wheelbarrow (a compound machine) and asked to determine what simple machines were used to form the wheelbarrow (an inclined plane, a wheel, an axle, and a lever).

Intermediate students studying ancient civilizations could be asked to construct a model of an ancient architectural site. First they would chose and research the site. Then they would submit an exhibit application, including a blueprint, a list of materials (and estimated cost), any special equipment needed, and an indication of which students will perform which tasks. After the teacher approves the application and the blueprint, students build their scale model. When the model is exhibited, they defend their representation, both orally and in writing, in terms of the environment and technological limitations of that era. There are self, peer, and teacher evaluations at the conclusion of the project.

> I like doing center activities. They are fun to do. They help me spell words, and do math and patterns. My favorite one has Legos.
>
> —*Denver Renner, dual language first grader*

> I think that counting little objects in first grade and kindergarten was a fun way to learn number concept. It has helped me in the third grade with addition, sub-

Process-Based Centers

traction, multiplication, and division. I have seen how much fun learning can turn into!

—*Carly Catherine Renner, dual language third grader*

Some of the most important educational tools I use in the classroom are multi-leveled content-area shelf activities that provide a variety of challenges for different types of learners. By providing these activities, I give the children the opportunity to work collaboratively or independently. The students are able to challenge themselves and as a result feel good about themselves and their accomplishments.

—*Dual language teacher and mentor at J. Marlan Walker International School*

Summary

Children learn best through personal experience and discovery. Children have a natural inner drive to manipulate and explore what is presented to them. Center activities are a venue for children to reach out, touch, and use their senses to learn. Their purpose is to encourage children to become independent workers and nurture in them a good self-image.

Assessing as a Way to Better Instruction and Accountability

What we want is to see the child in pursuit of knowledge and not knowledge in pursuit of the child.

—George Bernard Shaw

Journal Entry
February 8, 2005

My favorite assessment tool is the Assessment on the Run. How could I teach without this? I learn most about what my students know and are capable of doing by observing them engaged in their work. When I ask them what they are doing, why they are doing it, and what they have learned from doing the activity, I am able to plan where to take them next in their learning or where to return them to fill in gaps in their concept development.

—*Third-Grade Teacher*

As good ole Texas gals, we want to remind y'all of a li'l ole Texas proverb: You do not fatten the hog by weighing him. These days, when assessment is being emphasized above all else, this proverb is very appropriate. Nevertheless, assessment is certainly a highly valued and necessary step in the dual language immersion program and serves a threefold purpose: to determine instruction, monitor individual student progress, and demonstrate accountability.

The students in American dual language immersion schools have diverse economic backgrounds and ethnic heritages and include second language learners and those with other special needs. All are held to the same standards but require instruction designed to support their unique circumstances. States have developed standards, with attendant benchmarks and time lines, that each local school district must meet based on federal demands of accountability for individual student progress. The focus of current educational reform is to ensure each child masters the standards through instruction that addresses his individual needs. This instruction is not generic (because what is good for one is *not* good for all) but accommodates a variety of learning styles and special considerations. It follows that teachers must also use a broad range of authentic assessments to arrive at an accurate analysis of each individual student.

When teachers determine individual needs through authentic assessments, they can preside over a student-directed, teacher-facilitated classroom that stimulates students' innate desire to acquire new skills through collaboration. Some of our students are themselves marvelous teachers—and why shouldn't they be? They are fresh from the experience of learning and may perceive all of the stumbling blocks to comprehension better than an adult (Futrell 1998). The high point of a teacher's job is seeing the lightbulb turn on. It is through these observations that teachers become aware of students' abilities to problem solve, accomplish goals, and master learning objectives.

Norm-referenced assessments are required by the state to measure student performance. These types of tests are important in dual language immersion schools because they compare the test scores of immersion education students with the test scores of their age-group peers across the nation. Thomas and Collier (1997) have concluded that students who are educated in more than one language have cognitive benefits over students who learn via one language only.

Criterion-referenced assessments are required by states to measure student mastery of state standards. These tests are important because they are the data teachers need to plan their instruction. This planning is correlated with the standards and gives teachers an instructional focus that is both vertical and horizontal: vertical in that students acquire knowledge in sequence, building conceptual development on prior knowledge; horizontal in that teachers expect mastery of certain standards in previous grades and recognize that other standards will be mastered in subsequent grades.

When teachers give students opportunities to internalize a concept through concrete experience before asking them to apply the concept abstractly, the students' knowledge is easily demonstrated through standardized testing, provided students are prepared to take these kinds of tests—that is, when teachers include as part of their instruction test-taking strategies appropriate for the testing format.

An authentic assessment is one that allows teachers to determine what a student knows or is able to do. Its purpose is to show growth and inform instruction over a period of time. It is an alternative to traditional forms of one-shot testing that rely primarily on multiple-choice answers (O'Malley and Valdez-Pierce 1996). Authentic assessments are created and used by teachers in order to observe their students' growth and determine what additional practice they need in order to master grade-level objectives. It is only through authentic assessment that students learning in a second language are given the opportunity to demonstrate what they know. Traditional multiple-choice or fill-in-the-blank tests don't give students learning in a second language much of a chance to express their academic knowledge.

Authentic assessments include these defining characteristics:

- Rubrics specify specific criteria to be measured (see Figure 6–1).
- Content journals allow students to move from concrete experiences to abstract application. Following a hands-on activity, students record their learning process in the journal. Through these journals, teachers are able to assess students' critical-thinking skills.
- Assessment takes place on the run in anecdotal records (short accounts of interesting incidents) that include notes about each child's work ethic, attitudes, energy level, engagement, and home situation. These anecdotal records also include notes taken by the teacher as she observes the child participate in activities. The students' personal perceptions of their learning are revealed as they answer questions such as What are you doing? How are you doing it? and What have you learned from your work? An easy way to manage these notes is by taping index cards, in order, to the interior of both sides of a file folder bearing the student's name.
- Teacher-made tests determine student mastery of previously taught objectives. These tests can be multiple choice, fill in the blank, essay, and so on.
- Students are given the opportunity to exhibit their knowledge orally, through dramatic presentations, explanation of illustrations, reading workshop conferences, and role-plays. (These are usually graded, either by the teacher or other students, with a rubric.)

First-Grade Reading Rubric

Name _____

Reading Assignment _____

Concept of Print   _____/30
   • left to right (10 points)
   • return sweep (10 points)
   • one-to-one correspondence (10 points)

Uses Reading Strategies   _____/25
   • uses picture clues to identify words (5)
   • uses self-correcting strategies (5)
   • uses decoding skills (5)
   • identifies and reads sight words (5)
   • identifies beginning and ending sounds (5)

Fluency/Expression   _____/10
   • reads orally with fluency (5)
   • reads with expression (5)

Comprehension   _____/20
   • recalls details of text (5)
   • locates picture clues, words, and
     sentences to answer questions about the text (5)
   • responds to literature (5)
   • distinguishes between real and make-believe (5)

Figure 6–1. Sample Rubric

- Students evaluate their own behavior and work performance at the end of the day (see Figure 6–2). Through honest self-reflection, students see what they have accomplished and become intrinsically motivated.
- The teacher uses running records to determine individual students' fluency levels and then creates homogeneous groups for skill-based instruction. Here's how a reading record works. The teacher selects a leveled book and asks the child to read it aloud. The teacher records any reading fluency errors, as well as self-corrections, the child makes as he reads. The teacher then determines the student's independent, instructional, and frustration levels based on the accuracy of his reading.

Content-Based Journaling

Name _____

Week of _____

	M	T	W	Th	F
I followed directions.					
I completed all activities.					
I completed work neatly.					
I listened.					
I cooperated with my group.					

E
(EXCELLENT)

G
(GOOD)

NG
(NOT SO GOOD)

One goal I have for myself:

_____
_____
_____
_____

Figure 6–2. Sample Daily Evaluation

- Portfolios are created that include dated samples of student work illustrating the students' academic growth over time. These work samples provide students and teachers the data needed for self-reflection and assessment.
- The teacher asks higher-level questions that are geared to students' second language proficiency:
  - Students at the preproduction level of fluency respond by pointing or gesturing. For example, during a science unit on nutrition, the teacher asks students to put labeled visuals into categories of food types. Then the students select items for a balanced daily diet.
  - Students at the early production fluency level respond by naming, answering yes or no, or giving a one-word response. For example, during a science unit on insects, students are grouped in fours. These students take turns listing the body parts of an insect and then adding a one-word adjective to each body part. Students are then partnered.

Partner A describes an imaginary insect to partner B. Partner B draws the insect described. (Sharing these comical drawings brings humor into the classroom.)

- Students at the speech emergence fluency level respond in simple sentences. They are able to compare, describe, and sequence. For example, during a science unit on plants, students experiment with variables that alter plant growth and then write and illustrate a book that compares and contrasts the effects of the variables.

- Students at the intermediate fluency level respond by making predictions, describing situations, and narrating a sequence of events. For example, during a science unit on oceans, students, using research obtained via the library, technology, and interviews, predict what impact global warming will have on the coral reef off the coast of Australia.

Summary

Norm-referenced tests are a means to substantiate the benefits of a dual language immersion program. Over time, the data prove that this type of education is best for all students in public education and should not be used only in private or magnet settings. Criterion-referenced tests measure student progress and validate teachers' instruction. Through them teachers become aware of objectives and determine instructional methods needed for remediation or enrichment. Authentic assessment gives a true picture of what students are able to do. It removes the barrier of limited language proficiency and allows students to demonstrate their higher-level thinking skills. Through self-assessment, students reflect on their learning, become intrinsically motivated, and are stimulated to be lifelong learners.

And oh, yes: the fattest hogs are raised by the farmer who provides the most grub.

Building Community Support

Never doubt that a small group of thoughtful citizens can change the world. Indeed it is the only thing that ever has.

—Margaret Mead

Journal Entry
March 29, 2005

I remember that initially it was a chore to convince some parents that we would be able to teach the state standards to mastery as well as give bilingualism and biliteracy to their children as a bonus. Some were skeptical, how would the day be long enough to do both. We showed them the web planning of our units and we explained how Spanish was not taught as a foreign language but through immersion, and that in immersion education we have identified languages of instructional delivery. Again and again we repeated this and yet it was so foreign to their personal school experiences they could not understand. When I invited people to come see us in action then they were convinced. It just takes witnessing us in action to get what we do. The community becomes astonished at our results when they witness our children's ability to understand, to interact, to read, and write in two languages. Then they are amazed at how this happens. Our high performances on standardized assessment scores prove our academic success and our language growth shocks people.

—Dual Language Administrator

In recent years, public education has been negatively targeted in the news media. The current focus on improving test scores and identifying inadequate schools has resulted in a low opinion of our country's educational system. We can change public opinion, but only by helping our students acquire knowledge, not by making them memorize more facts. In a world of abundant information, students need to become researchers—to locate, analyze, and synthesize information. Our instruction needs to provide opportunities for students to compare and contrast, make choices, investigate, explore, collaborate, and problem solve.

Educators in dual language immersion programs become facilitators who prepare the proper environment and provide the proper tools so that students have the opportunity to become critical thinkers who can defend their opinions and justify their thought processes and are open-minded enough to value diverse opinions. Their instruction is student directed, not teacher directed.

The students are responsible for maintaining their space. Their teachers generate interest in topics through direct instruction and then provide resources students can use to investigate and enhance their understanding. This type of classroom can be foreign and difficult to understand for adults who were educated more traditionally.

It seems that the current nostalgic and romantic focus on reading, writing, and arithmetic is impeding our progress toward becoming the information-based society required by the twenty-first century. According to Toffler (2002), it took approximately fifty thousand years to accumulate the knowledge attributed to mankind in the year AD 1. It then took another fifteen hundred years to double that knowledge. But by the early 1970s, mankind was doubling its knowledge every six years. By 2012 human knowledge is expected to double every year. It seems obvious that instructional methods too must change. Teachers can no longer simply provide information; they must become the facilitators of student-directed classrooms, preparing students to become information processors, analysts, and self-motivated learners.

Community Involvement

Good public relations are essential if this paradigm shift in education is to be embraced. Only by knowing and understanding the purpose of a dual language immersion program will American citizens willingly accept, or better still *expect*, that their neighborhood school is nontraditional, one in which children learn in two languages, develop diplomacy skills, understand global economics, are introduced to and learn the latest technology, and develop an international outlook. The community will value this type of school if those who develop it treat it as a product that must be sold.

In order to promote schools like these, their proponents must

- seek out positive media coverage that
  - focuses on student achievement both in the local school and in other dual language immersion schools throughout the country
  - highlights innovative strategies used in the program such as hands-on activity centers
  - celebrates student presentations in both languages of instruction

- calls attention to special cultural events and assemblies
- explains partner planning and teaching
- advertises parenting classes
- provides examples of student-directed lessons
- interact with the community proactively:
  - interview CEOs and business owners to determine the job skills needed to work there
  - invite CEOs and business owners to speak to parent groups about these job skills
  - develop community partnerships to secure additional funds for special projects
  - invite community members to visit classrooms and observe the dual language immersion program at work
  - invite community bilingual businesspeople to come in and testify to how being bilingual has helped them succeed
  - invite a non-English-speaking guest to read to students or teach a short lesson
  - promote cultural awareness by inviting the public to school-sponsored performances by dancers, gymnasts, and storytellers
  - invite the community to student performances that feature all relevant languages
  - encourage reading throughout the community by loaning baskets of multilanguage books to local restaurants and doctors' and dentists' offices
  - create school and classroom websites and update them regularly with current events, information, activities, and achievements

Parental Support

The parents of children participating in dual language immersion programs must truly embrace the concepts of bilingualism, biliteracy, and biculturalism. They need to be able to support their children as they learn their second language. It is imperative that parents thoroughly understand the benefits their children receive from this type of education. The time spent on parent education will save teachers and administrators hours of time spent defending the program in individual conferences and solving individual problems.

Here are some possible ways to educate parents:

- Via the school newsletter, alert them to websites, articles, and books that address the cognitive advantages of bilingualism, discuss current and future real-world job skills, and celebrate successful dual language immersion programs.

- Prepare a brochure explaining the goals and methods of a dual language immersion school.
- Offer training and workshops in acquiring literacy in two languages, supporting their child at home even though they may not speak the second language themselves, working effectively with students in the classroom, and so on.
- Establish a parent-teacher support group to welcome new families to the school community, explain the curriculum, promote after-school activities, raise money, and encourage community relationships.
- Hold seminars in which parents can discuss and reflect on the purpose of dual language immersion. Topics could include
  - the role of foreign languages in national defense and the global economy
  - the disadvantages of monolingualism when half of the world's population is learning English as a second or third language
- Hold annual open houses and parent-teacher conferences.

Administrative Support

Dual language immersion programs demand administrative support and instructional leadership. Specifically, the school district and the local board of education must support the program by providing an equitable allocation of resources. Also, the principal needs to ensure that the program is integrated within the school as a whole and that all teachers and other school staff members understand the purpose and benefits of dual language immersion.

A dual language immersion program may be led by an assistant principal, program coordinator, or specialist teacher. This individual needs extensive knowledge about—and must value—the model of language education being implemented. Specifically, this person must know how second language develops; be conversant with immersion theory, research, instructional methods, and classroom practices; and perhaps most important, believe that the program works.

The administrator of a dual language immersion school must

- have the passion to lead the school community in a paradigm shift, educating students for the future, not the past
- be the public relations representative for the dual language immersion program
- ideally be bilingual, experienced in international travel, knowledgeable about world geography, and appreciative of other cultures

- hire qualified teachers who are familiar with the components of a dual language immersion program
- provide the necessary professional development to ensure the success of the dual language program
- recognize teacher candidates' ability to collaborate and cooperate as team players
- ensure that all members of the school staff believe in immersion programs and encourage those who do not to seek employment elsewhere
- ensure that the school's administrative offices are open, friendly, and welcoming and that staff members are able to explain the immersion program to anyone unfamiliar with the school
- support curricular extensions focusing on geography, literature, and the oral development of a third or fourth language
- be a problem solver who accepts challenges with flexibility and logical thinking

Teacher Support

Teachers in dual language immersion schools should have the appropriate academic credentials, know how to teach integrated content, be able to manage the classroom effectively, and be trained in dual language immersion. They should also be native to (or as proficient as a native in) their assigned language of instruction. Additionally, the teachers need to be dedicated and committed to the program. Because successfully implementing an immersion program requires teacher collaboration and hard work, teachers need to feel supported by administrators, parents, school specialists, and so forth.

Teachers need to display an enthusiasm for the program and share a common philosophy that all children can learn. The staff at the school must be united in support of the program. Without this unity, it will be more difficult to obtain the support of parents and the community at large. Ongoing communication between teachers, parents, administrators, and students is necessary if the program is to succeed.

Immersion teachers

- are enthusiastic, lifelong learners
- are inquisitive thinkers
- are flexible, open-minded, and willing to accept change
- are dedicated to using the best immersion instructional methods
- are willing to partner-teach
- are willing to share the responsibilities of instruction with a team partner

- are willing to share materials and collaborate with grade-level teams
- are moral, ethical, and responsible
- focus their energy on preparing the classroom and planning instruction
- dramatize their lessons to ensure their students understand
- are language role models
- reinforce students' intrinsic motivation
- possess cognitive and academic proficiency in the language of instruction
- are prepared to address parents' questions about instruction
- stay current on immersion research and discuss it with their colleagues
- keep parents informed about instructional methods, homework assignments, and ways they can help their children at home
- are willing and eager to participate in training sessions outside the normal school day
- display professionalism during parent-teacher meetings
- serve on committees for school improvement
- are able to develop integrated lessons for a thematic unit
- act as facilitators in a student-directed child-centered classroom
- know how to teach a balanced literacy program

Students

The students in dual language immersion schools receive a unique education that will prepare them to become lifelong learners able to adapt to future experiences. They benefit from a collaborative, synergistic school community in which all students are valued as thinkers, problem solvers, investigators, and researchers and are helped to reach their full potential.

Students in a dual language immersion program

- learn actively, through activity centers, cooperative learning, performances, and process-based instruction
- negotiate meaning while acquiring fluency in their second language by acting out, drawing pictures, mixing the two languages of instruction when speaking and writing, comparing and contrasting the known concept to the unknown concept, and using cognates
- complete assignments on schedule by setting weekly goals and managing their time
- develop a work ethic through teacher-facilitated and student-directed instruction that builds on intrinsic motivation; student activities are valued as work, not play
- are self-motivated because they own their learning

- develop life skills through cooperative learning, class meetings, negotiations at the peace table, and the responsibility of keeping their classroom organized
- are taught negotiation skills through compromise, self-reflection, peer mediation, and conflict resolution exercises and role-plays
- have the freedom to express their creativity through presentations and process-based centers because of their educators' fundamental respect for individuality
- develop self-esteem through accomplishment and empowerment
- become leaders through self-confidence and knowledge
- have the opportunity to debate and discuss
- evaluate what they have learned at the end of the day
- have opportunities to share their acquired knowledge with a variety of audiences: peers, teachers, administrators, school staff, family, and community members
- are encouraged to do research via library materials, technology, and interviews
- become team players via precooperative and cooperative learning structures that include equal participation and simultaneous interaction
- are culturally enriched via the in-depth integration of the five strands of geography: location, environment, movement of goods and people, economics, and governments
- have the cognitive advantages inherent in acquiring academic knowledge in more than one language

Community involvement is key to any successful dual language program. Its planning and implementation should include and be sensitive to parent concerns. The school community needs to be aware of the benefits provided by a dual language program. These benefits include cognitive advantages such as greater mental flexibility and problem-solving skills, which will increase future employment opportunities. Parental involvement and support can be provided in many ways—an open-door policy, adult instruction in the second language their children are learning, and a parent committee that provides support to families new to the school. Once parents see their child learning in another language there is 100 percent buy-in. But you have to get them in to see.

—*Alan Bowman, Principal, J. Marlan Walker International School*

Summary

By visiting international schools in El Paso, Texas; Seattle, Washington; and Shang Hai, China, we have come to realize the importance of visual presentation and public relations. Visitors entering these schools experience an environment rich in international symbols, like flags and student-made models of world-renowned architectural sites. The administrators proudly invite visitors to tour classrooms and hallways and experience the dual language model in action.

We have observed physical education classes conducted in the language representative of the activity: gymnastics in German, karate in Japanese, and ballet in Russian. At one school, the students were sharing their newly acquired knowledge with other students, teachers, parent helpers, and office staff by way of presentations supported by posters, models, dioramas, and student-made books. In the international school in China, Mandarin, Japanese, and English were the languages of instruction, and these three cultures had been infused into center activities (for example, the math centers included explorations with origami, the Japanese art of paper folding). The children in these schools were joyous and giggly. They greeted visitors with poise and self-confidence.

Why aren't educational institutions like these available for *all* children in the United States? The political issue of teaching children in more than one language is often misunderstood. The pro-American English-only advocates do not realize the disadvantages of an educational system limited to one language. Bilingual students have cognitive advantages over monolingual students: their comprehension is hastened and enhanced, they have greater opportunities for comparison and contrast, they are able to discern the meaning of more words, and they have greater problem-solving skills. *All* students benefit in a dual language immersion program, whether native Americans or immigrants from another country.

Conclusion
Embracing International
Dual Language Schools

*Do not confine your children to your own learning, for they
were born in another time.*

—Hebrew Prophet

Journal Entry
December 6, 2005
Today I observed in my grade level colleague's classroom. The students were
engaged in a seminar discussion on immigration patterns. They were comparing
and contrasting the movement of peoples in Australia, Canada and the United
States. I was amazed at their ability to ask and respond to inferential questions.
One student who had been researching immigration from Hong Kong to Australia
asked the question, "What experiences would a student have changing from a
school in Hong Kong to a school in Australia?" Another student was delighted by
the opportunity to share information he had read about schools in Australia. He
stated that because in Australia a social break for tea and cookies was provided in
mid afternoon the students emigrating from Hong Kong would have the opportunity to socialize and make new friends. The students all asked their teacher if they
could adopt this Australian practice into their own classroom.

—Second-Grade Teacher

We live in a global era that shapes world politics, commerce, the environment, and
international relations. Our increasingly connected world cries out for cultural
understanding and for the desire and the ability of different nationalities to communicate. The United States lags far behind other countries in second language
instruction and a knowledge of world geography. Other industrialized nations
require students to learn a second or a third language to better prepare for the future.

Currently there are a number of international dual language immersion schools in the United States that have begun to address multilingual and multicultural competencies required for the global job market. In these schools, students examine global issues, identify world problems, and grapple with international challenges. They recognize and analyze human differences and similarities. They compare and contrast the United States with other countries in the world.

International dual language immersion schools offer students a twenty-first-century curriculum focused on educating and preparing them to participate successfully in the global community and economy. That curriculum tends to concentrate on language, geography, global concepts and affairs, information analysis, communication skills, citizenship, technology, and career preparation.

Early exposure to a second language has been shown to increase students' native langauge skills and overall academic success. Some international schools give students the opportunity to learn content in a third language, which enhances their cognitive attainment even more.

International study often focuses on the five themes of geography: location, movement, environment, economics, and government. Students begin by learning about global geographical areas. They then examine immigration patterns in order to perceive the movement and interconnection of peoples and cultures. Through the study of the environment, students perceive the similarities and differences between disparate peoples. They also examine the differences between capitalism and communism and the interconnection of different nations' economies. Finally, students examine the similarities and differences between democracies, dictatorships, and monarchies.

Many schools' multicultural studies merely expose students to tourist geography limited to a nation's celebrations, cuisine, flag, and the like. International dual language immersion schools approach the topic in more depth, integrating five global concepts throughout the instruction:

1. *Culture*, the way of life of a group of people. People create environments and systems based on their own myths, values, traditions, and language in order to meet their basic human needs. Cultures are affected by physical environment and contacts with other societies.
2. *Interdependence*. The world is a system whose mechanisms interact to make a united, functioning whole.
3. *Power*, the ability to control. People and nations look to control others in order to impose their beliefs and values.
4. *Scarcity*. Humankind needs to balance what it needs and wants with the resources the earth provides. As more of the earth's resources become

limited, we need to determine how those resources are going to be distributed.

5. *Change*, making or becoming different over time.

International dual language immersion schools give students the opportunity to achieve academic excellence in all subject areas based on district, state, and national standards. Even more difficult than meeting the demands of challenging *subject matter* is creating a generation of highly skilled *learning activists*, students who singly or in groups identify and attack problems and seek skills as a function of habit and personality (Roberts and Staff of the National Paideia Center 1998). Students in international schools are challenged by way of seminar-like discussions with their teachers in which the students articulate, justify, and clarify their ideas. They are encouraged to use their higher-level thinking skills in order to problem solve and form opinions. Teaching like this requires active learners who listen, think, and contribute. It is essential for students to offer personal opinions and ask questions on the topic being studied.

Students in international dual language immersion schools also acquire the organizational and analytical skills necessary to research information, state their beliefs, and defend their conclusions in both languages of instruction. Before a seminar, students receive an outline of the upcoming lesson and are informed of the targeted objectives. Teachers deliver lessons using a logical structure that identifies and structures key concepts through graphic organizers and visuals. Through classroom and school performances, students develop the ability to communicate in distinct modes to diverse audiences and thus demonstrate their leadership skills. Access to information is increased through technology. Skills infused throughout the curriculum provide students the tools needed in a technological world. Computer skills are learned in connection with assignments in the content areas. Students research topics of interest; write about those topics; improve their vocabulary, reading, and spelling skills; and develop presentations using available software.

Students in international dual language immersion schools understand the connection between knowledge acquired inside a classroom and how that knowledge can be applied in everyday life. Through this enriched curriculum, students acquire the ability to analyze, synthesize, and evaluate ideas. Their practice with linking new information to known information prepares them for adult life and enhances their employment marketability. Most important, international school graduates become world citizens who respect others' points of view, form alliances to solve world problems, have the tools to realize their potential, and are able to travel without fear or inhibition.

World Travel Via the Internet

Portrait of an International School

The dual language immersion program described in this book was developed at the J. Marlan Walker International School, the first public international dual language immersion school in the state of Nevada, dedicated to providing a premium education that prepares students to become successful world citizens. The school, named for a respected community member who taught Spanish at the local high school for thirty-six years, opened in the fall of 2002, in Henderson, Nevada. The community has embraced this innovative program and curriculum and provided enormous support. The families feel privileged to have the opportunity for their children to attend this public international school.

The administrators were selected based on their knowledge of language acquisition, interest in geography, and extensive travels. Annette readily agreed to serve as assistant principal at the school's inception, seeing the opportunity to cap her career with dessert after she had been a good girl and had eaten all her vegetables (foreign language teacher, bilingual teacher, ESL teacher). Lore soon after became the school's consultant and teacher trainer. Half of the teachers hired for the primary grades were bilingual and biliterate.

In the first year only kindergarten students participated in the dual language immersion program. Grades 1 through 5 concentrated on the international studies curriculum. In the second year, first graders were added to the program, followed by an additional grade level each succeeding year. Currently, the program runs through grade 4.

Physical Environment

As one enters J. Marlan Walker International School, an impression of international studies is immediately apparent. Flags of the world adorn the vestibule, and windowed showcases display artifacts of diverse cultures and places traveled by Dr. Walker, the school's namesake.

On the right wall of the hallway leading from the vestibule, a large mural depicts the planet Earth wrapped in a ribbon of flags. This ribbon of flags continues throughout all of the hallways in the school, connecting intermittent murals representing the geographical themes included in the international curriculum. The Parent Teacher Organization donated the funds for this mural, and a local artist was commissioned to paint it. During the five months it took to create it, students observed the process and progress with great interest. It became a visual spark for their interest in world studies.

The school library continues the international theme, with country flags grouped by geographical theme. The library is filled with both English and Spanish materials: literature, reference books, software, and Websites; it includes a computer lab.

The school is a large rectangle with a courtyard in the center that shares a common glass wall with the corridors. The courtyard includes a stage and a portable microphone system for the presentation of student performances. This aesthetically pleasing parklike area, with trees, tables, and benches, is an appealing, low-stress environment in which to enjoy teaching and learning.

Academic Environment

The goals of the school are to develop social and academic competence in two or more languages; provide instruction that emphasizes high academic performance in all core subjects; and offer students ample opportunities to experience a variety of cultural studies through academics and the arts, communicate in diverse modes to a variety of audiences, engage in civic discourse, take action, and demonstrate leadership skills. Students are taught respect and appreciation for diversity. They become pen pals with students from other countries, use technology to acquire an

Mural Vignette Depicting Environmental Effects on Indigenous People

awareness of other cultures, compare and contrast other cultures with their own, role-play during sensitivity training sessions, and talk about diversity in seminars. This gives them a better understanding of self and others.

The immediate focus at all grade levels is thematic units integrating international studies. Via high-interest materials, students perceive the world as an interconnected entity while developing their reading and writing skills. The students become thoughtful, independent readers capable of in-depth comprehension. Using nonfiction literature, the students connect their reading to their background knowledge, create sensory images, ask questions, draw inferences, determine importance, synthesize ideas, and problem solve.

Each grade level focuses on one geographical theme:

1. In kindergarten and first grade, the theme is *location*. Students learn the names and locations of the continents and oceans, the hemispheres, the equator, and so on. They locate and identify places of the world where Spanish is spoken. They explore the people, fauna, and flora of Spain, Mexico, and Latin America. Students compare and contrast these countries with the United States.

2. In second grade, the theme is *movement*. Immigration patterns are followed, as is the transportation of goods in South Africa, Australia, and Canada. Students determine the changes brought about by movement. They compare and contrast these countries with the United States.

3. In third grade, the theme is *environment*. Students study the effects of environment upon selected Native American, African, and Amazonian tribes. Students perceive the similarities and differences among these disparate cultures.

4. In fourth grade, the theme is *economics*. By studying Nevada, the former USSR, and China, students perceive the differences between the economics of capitalism and communism as well as the interconnections between the economies of different nations.

5. In fifth grade, the theme is *government*. By studying the governments of England, Cuba, Saudi Arabia, and the United States, students perceive the similarities and differences between democracies, dictatorships, and monarchies.

As a parent of two children attending J. Marlan Walker International School, I have been fascinated watching my son, Joseph, acquire his second language without even realizing what is happening. Many times I have asked him how to say a specific word in Spanish. His response is always the same, "I don't know how to speak Spanish." Then one day when we were in a checkout line, a Spanish-speaking family in front of us was having a conversation. Joseph turned to me and said, "Their mom needs to know where the white socks are." I explained where they were, he translated what I had said to the mom, and off they went in the right direction. That was when I realized his language acquisition was happening in such a natural way he did not even notice his own progress. Rebekah, on the other hand, can hardly wait to speak multiple languages. She will tell me a word in English and then give me the word in a nonexistent language saying it is Spanish. When I tell her it does not sound like Spanish, she tells me she would know because she is the one who speaks Spanish, not me! I must admit she's got me there!

—*Eva M. White, Parent, J. Marlan Walker International School*

Appendix A
Stages of Language Acquisition

Stage 1: Preproduction

Students *have*
- minimal comprehension
- no verbal production

Students *can*
- nod answers to questions
- draw cartoons and pictures
- point to objects or print
- move to show understanding
- categorize objects or pictures
- match words or objects
- pantomime
- role-play

Teachers *should*
- provide ample listening opportunities
- create a classroom dripping with language
- use mixed-ability groupings
- create high context for shared reading
- use physical movement, art, mime, and music

Stage 2: Early Production

Students *have*
- limited comprehension
- one- and two-word responses

Students *can*
- identify people, places, and things
- list and categorize
- repeat memorable language

- listen with greater understanding
- use routine expressions independently

Teachers *should*
- ask yes-or-no, either-or, and *who, what,* and *where* questions
- continue to provide listening opportunities with rich context
- have students complete sentences with one- or two-word responses
- have students label or manipulate pictures and objects
- do "shared reading" with props, building upon students' prior knowledge
- use predictable and patterned books
- introduce "dialogue journals" (supported by conversation)

Stage 3: Speech Emergence

Students *have*
- good comprehension
- enough proficiency to make simple sentences (with errors)

Students *can*
- describe events, places, and people
- define new vocabulary
- recall facts
- retell information from text
- explain academic concepts
- summarize
- compare and contrast

Teachers *should*
- ask open-ended questions
- model, expand, restate, and enrich student language
- have students describe personal experiences
- use predictable or patterned books for shared and guided reading
- support the use of content-area texts with retellings, role-playing, and so forth
- have students create books through "language experience" activities

Stage 4: Intermediate Fluency

Students *have*
- excellent comprehension
- few grammar errors

Students *can*

- give opinions
- debate with others
- justify views or behaviors
- defend actions and opinions
- negotiate with others
- persuade
- express the results of synthesis, analysis, and evaluation

Teachers *should*

- structure group discussions
- guide the use of reference materials
- provide more advanced literature
- ask students to create narratives
- provide for a variety of realistic writing opportunities
- publish students' writing

Stage 5: Advanced Fluency

Students *have*

- near-native speech

Students *can*

- produce written and oral language that is comparable to that of native English speakers of the same age

Teachers *should*

- continue ongoing language development through integrated language arts and content-area activities

Appendix B
Strategies for Language Acquisition

1. Label objects in the room.
2. Teach with plenty of visual cues:
   a. pictures
   b. maps
   c. diagrams
   d. real objects
   e. graphic organizers
3. Talk with gestures and facial expressions and use pantomime.
4. Make input more comprehensible to the students.
   a. Use slow rate of speech.
   b. Use frequent pauses.
   c. Use students' names.
   d. Use shorter sentences and phrases.
   e. Avoid the use of slang or idiomatic speech.
   f. Enunciate clearly.
   g. Emphasize key words.
   h. Rephrase and restate information.
5. Pair students with different primary languages.
6. Pair students new to the program with veteran students.
7. Place new students near the teacher.
8. Focus on meaning and comprehension rather than on correcting grammatical errors.
9. Check frequently for comprehension.
10. Give clear directions.
11. Model, show, and demonstrate.
12. Create an authentic context in which students have to negotiate meaning:
    a. dramatic play
    b. seminar discussions
    c. debate
13. Allow students to share their personal experiences.
    a. Ask them to write about them.

b. Hold seminar discussions.

c. Elicit prior knowledge.

14. Provide bilingual classroom dictionaries with visuals in which students can look up new words.

15. Teach students metacognitive strategies.

Appendix C
Thematic Unit

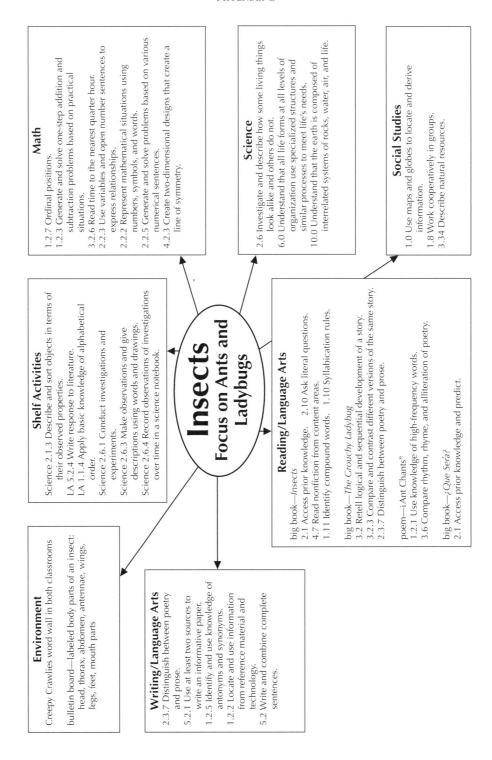

Insects
Focus on Ants and Ladybugs

Math
1.2.7 Ordinal positions.
1.2.3 Generate and solve one-step addition and subtraction problems based on practical situations.
3.2.6 Read time to the nearest quarter hour.
2.2.3 Use variables and open number sentences to express relationships.
2.2.2 Represent mathematical situations using numbers, symbols, and words.
2.2.5 Generate and solve problems based on various numerical sentences.
4.2.3 Create two-dimensional designs that create a line of symmetry.

Science
2.6 Investigate and describe how some living things look alike and others do not.
6.0 Understand that all life forms at all levels of organization use specialized structures and similar processes to meet life's needs.
10.0 Understand that the earth is composed of interrelated systems of rocks, water, air, and life.

Social Studies
1.0 Use maps and globes to locate and derive information.
1.8 Work cooperatively in groups.
3.34 Describe natural resources.

Shelf Activities
Science 2.1.3 Describe and sort objects in terms of their observed properties.
LA 5.2.4 Write response to literature.
LA 1.1.4 Apply basic knowledge of alphabetical order.
Science 2.6.1 Conduct investigations and experiments.
Science 2.6.3 Make observations and give descriptions using words and drawings.
Science 2.6.4 Record observations of investigations over time in a science notebook.

Reading/Language Arts
big book—*Insects*
2.1 Access prior knowledge.   2.10 Ask literal questions.
4.7 Read nonfiction from content areas.   1.10 Syllabication rules.
1.11 Identify compound words.

big book—*The Grouchy Ladybug*
3.2 Retell logical and sequential development of a story.
3.2.3 Compare and contrast different versions of the same story.
2.3.7 Distinguish between poetry and prose.

poem—"¡Ant Chants"
1.2.1 Use knowledge of high-frequency words.
3.6 Compare rhythm, rhyme, and alliteration of poetry.

big book—*¿Que Será?*
2.1 Access prior knowledge and predict.

Environment
Creepy Crawlies word wall in both classrooms
bulletin board—labeled body parts of an insect: head, thorax, abdomen, antennae, wings, legs, feet, mouth parts

Writing/Language Arts
2.3.7 Distinguish between poetry and prose.
5.2.1 Use at least two sources to write an informative paper.
1.2.5 Identify and use knowledge of antonyms and synonyms.
1.2.2 Locate and use information from reference material and technology.
5.2 Write and combine complete sentences.

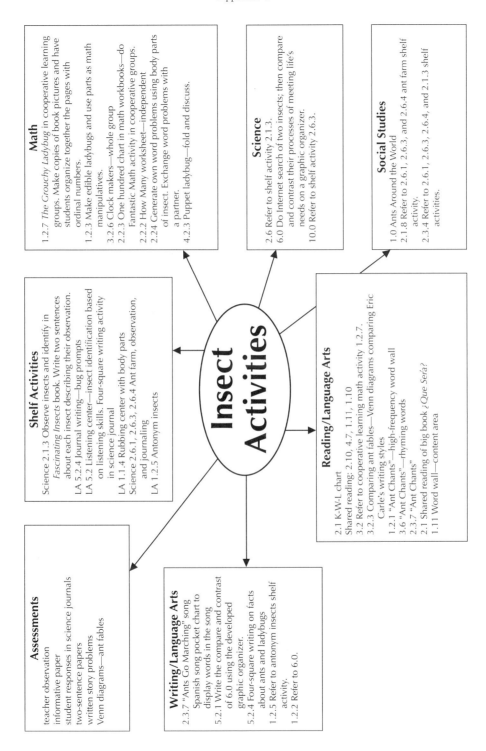

Insect Activities

Math

1.2.7 *The Grouchy Ladybug* in cooperative learning groups. Make copies of book pictures and have students organize together the pages with ordinal numbers.
1.2.3 Make edible ladybugs and use parts as math manipulatives.
3.2.6 Clock makers—whole group
2.2.3 One hundred chart in math workbooks—do Fantastic Math activity in cooperative groups.
2.2.2 How Many worksheet—independent
2.2.4 Generate own word problems using body parts of insect. Exchange word problems with a partner.
4.2.3 Puppet ladybug—fold and discuss.

Science

2.6 Refer to shelf activity 2.1.3.
6.0 Do Internet search of two insects; then compare and contrast their processes of meeting life's needs on a graphic organizer.
10.0 Refer to shelf activity 2.6.3.

Social Studies

1.0 Ants Around the World
2.1.8 Refer to 2.6.1, 2.6.3, and 2.6.4 ant farm shelf activity.
2.3.4 Refer to 2.6.1, 2.6.3, 2.6.4, and 2.1.3 shelf activities.

Shelf Activities

Science 2.1.3 Observe insects and identify in *Fascinating Insects* book. Write two sentences about each insect describing their observation.
LA 5.2.4 Journal writing—bug prompts
LA 5.2 Listening center—insect identification based on listening skills. Four-square writing activity in science journal
LA 1.1.4 Rubbing center with body parts
Science 2.6.1, 2.6.3, 2.6.4 Ant farm, observation, and journaling
LA 1.2.5 Antonym insects

Reading/Language Arts

2.1 K-W-L chart
Shared reading: 2.10, 4.7, 1.11, 1.10
3.2 Refer to cooperative learning math activity 1.2.7.
3.2.3 Comparing ant fables—Venn diagrams comparing Eric Carle's writing styles
1.2.1 "Ant Chants"—high-frequency word wall
3.6 "Ant Chants"—rhyming words
2.3.7 "Ant Chants"
2.1 Shared reading of big book ¿*Que Será*?
1.11 Word wall—content area

Writing/Language Arts

2.3.7 "Ants Go Marching" song Spanish song pocket chart to display words in the song
5.2.1 Write the compare and contrast of 6.0 using the developed graphic organizer.
5.2.4 Four-square writing on facts about ants and ladybugs
1.2.5 Refer to antonym insects shelf activity.
1.2.2 Refer to 6.0.

Assessments

teacher observation
informative paper
student responses in science journals
two-sentence papers
written story problems
Venn diagrams—ant fables

References

Allport, G. 1954. *The Nature of Prejudice*. Cambridge, MA: Addison Wesley.

Asher, J. 1986. *Learning Another Language Through Actions: The Complete Teacher's Guide*. Los Gatos, CA: Sky Oaks.

Bronowski, J. 1974. *The Ascent of Man*. Boston: Little, Brown.

Brophy, J. 1986. "Teacher Influences of Student Achievement." *American Psychologist* 41: 1069–77.

Cloud, N., F. Genesee, and E. Hamayan. 2000. *Dual Language Instruction: A Handbook for Enriched Education*. Boston: Heinle and Heinle.

Cummins, J. 1979. "Linguistic Interdependence and the Educational Development of Children." *Review of Educational Research* 49: 222–51.

———. 1987. *Bilingualism, Language Proficiency, and Metalinguistic Development*. Hillsdale, NJ: Lawrence Erlbaum.

———. 1992. "Bilingual Education and English Immersion: The Ramirez Report in Theoretical Perspective." *The Journal of the National Association for Bilingual Education* 16 (1–2): 91–104.

Cunningham, P. M. 1995. *Phonics They Use: Words for Reading and Writing*. New York: HarperCollins.

Diaz, R. M., C. J. Neal, and M. Amaya-Williams. 1990. "The Social Origins of Self Regulation." In *Vygotsky and Education: Instructional Implication and Application of Sociohistorical Psychology*, ed. L. Moll, 127–54. New York: Cambridge University Press.

Dragan, P. 2005. *A How-to Guide for Teaching English Language Learners: In the Primary Classroom*. Portsmouth, NH: Heinemann.

Dusek, J. B. 1985. *Teacher Expectations*. Hillsdale, NJ: Lawrence Erlbaum.

Edelsky, C. 1982. "Writing in a Bilingual Program." *TESOL Quarterly* 16: 211–28.

Faltis, C. 1997. *Joinfostering: Adapting Teaching for the Multilingual Classroom*. Upper Saddle River, NJ: Prentice Hall.

Fletcher, R., and J. Portalupi. 2001. *Writing Workshop: The Essential Guide*. Portsmouth, NH: Heinemann.

Freeman, Y. S., D. E. Freeman, and S. Mercuri. 2005. *Dual Language Essentials for Teachers and Administrators*. Portsmouth, NH: Heinemann.

Freeman Dhority, L., and E. Jensen. 1998. *Joyful Fluency: Brain-Compatible Second Language Acquisition*. San Diego: Brain Store.

Futrell, K. 1998. *The Normalized Child*. Cleveland, OH: North American Montessori Teachers Association.

Galassi, A. 2002. *Reading at Home Folders (RAH, RAH)*. Henderson, NV.

Genesee, F. 1984. *Historical and Theoretical Foundations of Immersion Education*. Sacramento: California State Department of Education.

———. 1987. *Learning Through Two Languages*. Cambridge, MA: Newbury House.

Graves, D. 1991. *Build a Literate Classroom*. Portsmouth, NH: Heinemann.

Harvey, S., and A. Goudvis. 2000. *Strategies That Work: Teaching Comprehension to Enhance Understanding*. Ontario, Canada: Pembroke.

Hudelson, S. 1984. "Kan yu ret an rayt en ingles: Children Become Literate in English as a Second Language." *TESOL Quarterly* 18 (2): 221–37.

Jackson, Linda. 2005. *ADAPTA Teachers' Guides*. San Antonio, TX: Early Learning Materials.

Jensen, E. 1995. *Super Teaching*. San Diego: Brain Store.

Johnson, D. W., and R. T. Johnson. 1999. *Learning Together and Alone: Cooperative, Competitive, and Individualistic Learning*. Boston: Allyn and Bacon.

Keene, E. O., and S. Zimmermann. 1997. *Mosaic of Thought*. Portsmouth, NH: Heinemann.

Krashen, S., and T. Terrell. 1983. *The Natural Approach*. San Francisco: Alemany.

Lambert, W. E. 1984. "An Overview of Issues in Immersion Education." In *Studies in Immersion Education: A Collection for U.S. Educators*, 8–30. Sacramento: California State Department of Education.

Lindholm, K. J. 1992. *Two Way Bilingual/Immersion Education: Theory, Conceptual Issues and Pedagogical Implications*. Tempe, AZ: Bilingual Press.

Linney, J. A., and E. Seidman. 1989. "The Future of Schooling." *American Psychologist* 44: 336–40.

McCloskey, M. L. 1999. "Scaffolding for Reading: Providing Support Through the Reading Process." *ESL* (Nov./Dec.).

Montague, N. S. 1997. "Critical Component for Dual Language Programs." *Bilingual Research Journal* 21 (4): 409–17.

Nanez, J., and R. Padilla. 1995. "Bilingualism and Processing of Elementary Cognitive Tasks by Chicano Adolescents." *Bilingual Research Journal* 19 (2): 249–60.

O'Malley, J. M., and L. Valdez-Pierce. 1996. *Authentic Assessment for English Language Learners*. New York: Addison-Wesley-Longman.

Peal, E., and W. E. Lambert. 1962. "The Relations of Bilingualism to Intellectual Intelligence." *Psychological Monographs* 76: 1–23.

Pertzman, F., and G. Gadda. 1991. *Guidelines for Teaching a Sheltered Content Class with Different Eyes: Insight into Teaching Language Minority Students Across the Disciplines.* Cambridge, MA: Addison-Wesley.

Roberts, T., and the Staff of the National Paideia Center. 1998. *The Power of Paideia Schools: Defining Lives Through Learning.* Alexandria, VA: Association for Supervision and Curriculum Development.

Routman, R. 2005. *Writing Essentials: Raising Expectations and Results While Simplifying Teaching.* Portsmouth, NH: Heinemann.

Slavin, R. E. 1983. *Cooperative Learning.* New York: Longman.

Thomas, W., and V. Collier. 1997. *School Effectiveness for Language Minority Students.* Washington, DC: National Clearinghouse for Bilingual Education.

Toffler, A. 2002. "Communications Revolution Just Waiting to Happen." www.indrainfoline.com. Retrieved March 7, 2005.

Tompkins, G. 1997. *Literacy for the 21st Century: A Balanced Approach.* Upper Saddle River, NJ: Merrill, Prentice-Hall.

Troike, R. C. 1978. "Research Evidence for the Effectiveness of Bilingual Education." *NABE Journal* 3: 13–24.

Vygotsky, L. S. 1978. *Mind in Society: The Development of Higher Psychological Processes.* Cambridge, MA: MIT Press.

———. 1986. *Thought and Language.* Cambridge, MA: MIT Press.

Walter, T. 1996. *Amazing English! How-to Handbook.* Cambridge, MA: Addison-Wesley.

Wertsch, J. 1985. *Culture, Communication and Cognition: Vygotskian Perspectives.* New York: Cambridge University Press.

Willig, A. 1985. "A Meta-Analysis of Selected Studies on the Effectiveness of Bilingual Education." *Review of Educational Research* 55: 269–317.

Wink, J., and L. G. Putney. 2002. *A Vision of Vygotsky.* Boston: Allyn and Bacon.

Index